CONSUELO SAAH BAEHR

Report
from the Heart

SIMON AND SCHUSTER · NEW YORK

1 2 3 4 5 6 7 8 9 10

Library of Congress Cataloging in Publication Data

Baehr, Consuelo Saah.
  Report from the heart.
    1. Baehr, Consuelo Saah.   2. Housewives—Personal narra-
tives. I. Title.
HQ759.B23   301.42'7'0924   76-2517
ISBN 0-671-22262-7

For D.

I would like to thank Dr. Albert Ellis for permission to use his name and to reconstruct some of our conversations, real and imagined.

I would also like to thank my children, Andrew, Nicholas and Amanda, for their admirable and touching behavior at certain times during the writing of this book. I hope the revelations are useful to them in later life.

Introduction

THIS IS NOT A NOVEL or a fictionalized account of an existing situation. It *is* the existing situation. The children mentioned, Andrew, Nicholas and Amanda, exist. They are my children. The husband, D., exists. He is my husband. The woman, the narrator, is me at a certain point in my life just prior to writing this book. The house I describe is our house, a house we built and still inhabit.

The friends, neighbors and other voices in the book are real in that they exist, what they say has been said, what they do has been done, but the names are not their names and sometimes one person is a composite of two or more personalities.

Some of the conversations in the book are verbatim accounts of actual conversations. Others are reconstructions of several conversations distilled into one. I did not invent any dialogue. It was all said, including what the children say.

The mystic (now deceased) was a spiritual teacher (my spiritual teacher), whose home base was California and who visited the New York area once or twice a year. He did hold classes in the Laurelton Room of the Hotel Wellington and I did attend.

The action takes place in one day, an ordinary day in our life.

CSB

Chapter One

6:24 BY THE DIGITAL CLOCK, a stark futuristic affair set down on a wobbly antique child's worktable, the only wobbly note in an otherwise well-planned, enviable bedroom.

I do not like to be left sleeping behind a closed door, and while D., my husband, knows this, every once in a while (this morning) he'll be very careful up to that point not to wake me but then suddenly pull the heavy door after him carelessly as he goes off to jog. When I first met him he ran in place; now, ten years later, he jogs a metered quarter-mile track. Who knows but that some day he'll try for open country? We move slowly, both of us. Very slowly. Unless you believe in an afterlife, in which case we're moving very fast.

Other mornings he wakes me in more gentle ways, hoisting the covers up about me and carefully folding the sheet over the blanket so the wool won't irritate my face. After all, I am the mother of his children.

I tell him my father used to do that and add slyly, "Why aren't you stingier? Then you'd be *just* like my daddy." He smiles defensively. Such subterranean truths, if told at all, should not be spilled in passing.

We are true children of the age. We know all about Daddy love, Mother hate, complicated sexual longings, etc., etc., but we still hold a lot in. Our book of revelation is a slim volume and very unrevealing.

Calling out quickly sometimes gets him back after the door

has clunked shut but sometimes not, and if it does get him back he won't remember my telling him any such thing, and for a moment I'll wonder if I've really told him or just thought it as I've thought so many other things that should have been said but weren't.

This morning, I'm opening the door myself and crawling back to bed. I am not yet the benign, amorphous cookie-maker. Today, I have a chore facing me that, even as I think of it, makes the room feel sultry, though it's only mid-April. Today, I must make as many telephone calls as it takes to round up six guests for this Saturday because we owe everybody and haven't had anyone in since last December.

Each Saturday night for the last four months, D. and I lie in our king-size bed and watch the Mary Tyler Moore show and then the Bob Newhart show. By the time the Carol Burnett show comes on, D. will rise with what I take to be a mixture of boredom and disgust and mutter "What's it all about?" before moving to the living room to read his investment advice on selecting options, longs and shorts. After that, he reads the Saturday *Times* until it is late enough to go to bed.

Here in Lattingtown, on the North Shore of Long Island, in the state of New York, where we live, we call on Tuesday for Saturday dinner—usually, however, two to three weeks in advance. So at this late date I will probably not get my first choice or my second but perhaps the third, which will be the Riddleys (third simply because we don't owe them a dinner, they being sound and likeable people who are invited often because they go with everyone).

It takes some courage to call this late. It will cross minds that we are caught free on a Saturday night, which in itself is not damaging, but when it is coupled with other thoughts about Her (meaning me)—that lately she is vague and given to *non sequiturs*, going on and on about the ills of the American diet and how refined sugar is the real killer, causer of rowdy children, slow learners, bad moods and mental aberrations—then an interesting picture begins to emerge of troubles, anxiety, a deep and unfixable something. Interesting, speculative thoughts will crackle over the airwaves, although D. would say I'm being paranoid. That I'm well liked, possibly envied, in our community.

The real-estate ads refer to our community as horse country, the fabled estate-dotted Gold Coast of Long Island. Despite the ads, the area is too beautiful for satire, much of it rolling country in its natural wooded state. There really *are* horses, plus a few farms and, of course, the sea.

"It is the kind of atmosphere money can't buy," drawl the realtors in their best North Shore lockjaw, but in fact it *has* been bought up and locked away by very old money. When you drive through our villages, there are signs everywhere to shut out the non-belongers. No parking on any street in this village. No stopping, No outlet. (Who wants to plug in? shrugs a mystified friend from New Jersey.) Members only. No trespassing. Before we lived here, when we were scouting the neighborhood, D. would add: No wishing. No looking. No daydreaming.

We live in an upper middle class development that used to be the entire estate of J. P. Morgan's lawyer, a man named Guthrie. Three winding country roads (where Mrs. Guthrie used to toot around in her electric car) are entered from the main road through huge iron gates and lead to a creek and boat basin. A few yards beyond is a swimmable stretch of Long Island Sound.

Our house, designed by D., is on a not-quite-wild, exquisite setting of dogwood, black birch, beech, tulip and oak trees that seem to suffocate us in the summer and stand naked all winter gossiping about my life. They are content to leave D. alone; after all, he comes home to these woods, these stars, these *rarae aves* as a thirsty man rushes to a clear, promising stream. I, on the other hand, have come to distrust seclusion and, by extension, my immediate surroundings. He's always looking up at the night for shooting stars, for satellites, for UFO's.

"Do you know," he says, "that if a twin traveled into space, he'd return a younger man than the twin that stayed behind on earth?"

"I don't know any twins," I reply. "The only grown-up twins I know of are John Lindsay and his brother and I never saw the brother." He tells me that the moon rises and sets like the sun and I snicker and ask if anyone besides himself is aware of it.

D. and I, neither old nor very rich, live on the middle road, very close to the beach where we go every day except in the dead of winter when the children can't take it. D. says the water and beach are different every day. It looks the same to me. It is a tragicomic pull between us that he loves nature and I (the drama of birth being *fini*) can take it or leave it.

There are still remnants of formal plantings around the beach, hedges that were once elaborately sculpted and other plantings that show great imagination. Two rambling groves of rose hips still bloom profusely and produce an abundance of fruit. There is a path between the beach and the creek lined with beach plum and, behind that, scrub pine, yucca and cactus.

Wild asparagus are growing in front of the dunes and, while I haven't yet seen them, I know they're there for the picking. A lady enamelist who lived in one of the beach-front houses harvested them every spring until she moved away. Once D. and I met her coming from the path and both her hands were stretched tight across two bunches of asparagus.

"Here's my supper," she said, clutching her booty. "They're wild. I pick them every spring."

"Who planted them?"

"The birds. The birds scatter the seeds."

When we asked where they were, she smiled and wagged her head. The enamelist is gone now and every spring D. and I look for the asparagus and wonder how she is doing and what she is enameling and regret deeply not getting the Great Asparagus Secret.

When I had learned the secret of imagining from the mystic, one of the first things I imagined was finding the wild asparagus patch. I saw myself coming upon it all alone and being surprised because I hadn't been looking for it. I began to jump up and down, flapping my arms as I do when I'm frightened or startled or when I'm very, very happy.

Until recently, I was ready and able to give small parties for eight around our round oak table, and I remained excited and vivacious throughout. But afterward, especially if it had gone well, such gloom and doom. It had to do with the feeling, instilled God knows when, that we women, the girls, the ladies, have been preparing for these glorious dinner parties since we were tiny females learning to kiss our Daddies and twist our little bottoms and put our noses in the air. And now, when these occasions crop up, we have to put two and two together. Drag out the adding machine and say to ourselves: Well, what have we got here? How are we doing? There's the husband, the house, the skinny Bendel shirt, the palazzo pants, the espadrilles, the sterling silver bean bobbing nervously between scant breasts, the three children slipping and sliding on the oak floor in their Saf-T-Feet jammies—and then later realizing the goals were inappropriate. As with eating Chinese food, the spirit is hungry again an hour later.

Now the thought of giving one of our pleasant parties (or going to one for that matter) paralyzes me and I don't think it is laziness or immaturity or a tendency to hypoglycemia. I am in the grip of inactivity. In my thirty-ninth year with everything in the world to look forward to or indeed to inspect right now, I don't want to do anything. Lately, the events of my mornings, nights, dusks and dawns are no more than relay sticks handed from me to me to remind myself which portion of the race I am running. I lead a rich inner life (ha, ha). It's as simple as that. No really big scoops, mind you. No same-gender lover waiting in the wings. No double life, no secret drinking. Secret eating, yes! And a distillation of the second string thoughts that increasingly have their

15

way in my head would certainly give a more accurate picture of our (my) life than what is passing for my life.

•

I began going to the mystic right after George Van Allen's New Year's Eve party, during which I hid in a coat closet at midnight, not wishing to kiss or be kissed by the Puerto Rican actress-singer who had just been accepted to the Actor's Studio, nor the airline labor biggie who came with the chubby blonde in a diaphanous apricot gown, nor the South American playboy wearing a bouclé knit shirt-jac and an expandable metal watchband, both of which, to me, are fashion no-no's.

George Van Allen, the sole bachelor in our neighborhood, has two factions at his parties. First, there are the neighbors: stiff, successful, cheerfully dressed. Then there are George's "outside" friends: slinky, long-haired, unattached, on the fringes of things, fantastic dancers, unneedy of conversation, content to sway the evening away.

What drove me to the mystic, however, had nothing to do with the people. There was something else. There was a huge built-in fish tank that was half outdoors and half part of the house. You could see the fish through a huge glass wall, and that day the heating element had failed and ice had formed. We were warned by gregarious, hyperactive George that the undue pressure might cause the inner glass to give way. But even more provocative, to me, was the idea of the fish being imprisoned in the glass. Sealed in. Even though I know right well that this is a natural state for fish and they feel no discomfort, my sense of their suffocation became so intense I had to leave quickly, whispering something to D. about my period.

It wasn't only George's iced-over fish tank, however handily symbolic, that made me feel closed up, suffocating, but everything else in general—the meat bins at Shop-Rite, the meat itself, especially the beef, the frozen food aisle, our hall closet full of dusty galoshes. My eldest son. Clearly my spirits

16

needed hyping up and there was no parish priest, no family doctor, no trusted long-time counselor. So I found myself a mystic. I wanted a little magic, I suppose.

A few mornings later, I was pleased to see the little ad in the Saturday *Times* about the mystic's being in town, and I made arrangements to attend the lectures, even though it was very hard for me to get away, the children being so little (seven, four and three).

I attended the lectures three times a week for two weeks in the Laurelton Room of the Hotel Wellington near Carnegie Hall. Since then, over two months now, I have been doing all of the mental exercises the mystic taught us, including the one where I see myself as thin as I wish to be, content, energetic, getting along with the children. Each time I breathe deeply, I say quietly but firmly to myself (and this is my own improvisation), "All the resentment and feelings of helplessness are being exhaled out of me and I am breathing in energy, enthusiasm and power."

I had been to the mystic ten years before when I was single, and he had helped me then, although I can't now remember what the problem had been. The same is true now. I don't know what the problem is, although I'm very familiar with the symptoms, which I will try to relate.

I do not tell anyone about the mystic, although he's quite acceptable as a spiritual leader. A proper Englishman from Barbados who left a family fortune to go his own way. Put him in an alb, a minister's robe and he'd appease anyone. But my mystic doesn't hem and haw about life's promises, about the love of God for me. He tells me outrageous things that I love to hear—that I have a hand in my own creation. To me, this is a small sign of hope in an otherwise closed-up world.

•

There is someone standing outside my door. I hear the soft breathing, more like a sigh. Tiny, premeditated sighs. They (the children) can be so daring all day and now so reverential of my sleep. "Come in, whoever it is." It is Andrew, my eldest.

"Mom, I don't have any socks in the drawer."

"Look in the dryer. And scrape the sides. Sometimes they stick to the sides. You have to wear your sneakers today, too. It's gym day."

"I wear my sneakers every day now because we play kickball at recess."

"You know how to play kickball?" Suddenly I'm curious as to what's happening at school. For a long time I didn't want to think about stubby fingers jiggling lunch money in shallow pockets, carrying trays of food in the cafeteria. I didn't want to know if he were trying to sit still, trying to take orders from strangers. But now, I want to know.

"Where do you play? In the gym?"

"Out. Unless the ground's too wet, then we have to stay on the blacktop or indoors."

"And you're on a team?"

"Yeah . . ." He says it reluctantly. "But I'm not always picked for a team."

"Why not?"

"I don't know." I know. A jab of guilt goes through me. He has been skipped a grade and it hasn't worked out in every way.

"Well, you must know. Maybe you don't know all the rules yet and they don't want to take the time to show you."

"No . . . that isn't it." He dismisses my suggestion, as he should. Why can't I leave him alone with his problem instead of handing him phony solutions.

"What do you do when you're not picked?"

"When we first go out and I see I'm not going to be picked, I make believe I'm under a magic spell and then I make up rules for the magic spell; I can only go on the slide three times, then on each swing three times, then walk around the building three times and I'm free of the spell." He's suddenly embarrassed and stops.

"Andrew, do you wish you could be back in the first grade?"

"Oh, no. That's too easy for me." He's parroting something he's heard. Probably from me.

"But wouldn't that be nice, to relax and have things easy for a change."

"Uh huh." He leaves in search of his socks.

This magic spell business is not new. He used to have an imaginary friend named Alice, before Nicholas, my second son, was born. Alice went everywhere with him. Ate with us. Slept at the foot of his bed. We had to be careful not to step on her, not to hurt her feelings. Once he came home from nursery school and told me the door of the bus had closed before Alice could get on. I had to drive back to the school to get her. He spotted her on the road and said very calmly, "There she is now. She was walking home." He was obviously proud of her initiative. Alice is in Barbados now. He left her there without explanation the winter he was four. We were on the plane before take-off and, suddenly, with a sense of panic, with visions of having to stop the plane and explain to the pilot that we had forgotten Alice, I brought it up.

"Where's Alice?"

"Oh, I left her at the hotel."

"You're not bringing her home with us?"

"No. She likes it here. It's summer all the time." That was the last we heard of Alice.

So that's his way, I think, this A-One Reader, who's too smart for his own good, who goes inside when the going gets rough. Just like his mother. Andrew wouldn't see it that way. "Children are different," he's always advising me. When we're discussing how we could improve things between us, he tells me soberly that I yell at them for nothing. Dreamily looking off into the distance, letting crumbs of bread linger on his lips, he says, "You yell at us for nothing."

"Not for nothing." I'm quick to defend myself (a tactical error D. warns me, implying we are both on equal footing).

"Every day no one wants to eat what I cook. If it were really terrible, your father would tell me. He likes it but you children don't. Why is that?"

"He's a grown-up," he answers with perfect logic, "and we're children. We're different. Children are different."

Andrew is so at home with truth I'm tempted to ask him other things as well. Why the best good times are unplanned. Why I seem to be waiting for something and incapable of starting my life in earnest. And he'd answer me, too, I have no doubt of that, but at the same time he'd be onto me so quickly and either give me a sly answer or trick me or use his knowledge as a weapon. Nothing is simple between us. Or, if it is simple, we're not content to leave it at that. We (or perhaps just I) want to take it further and wring some guarantee out of it that can be tucked away for future reference. In the end, everything is complicated and unresolved. He's seven.

It's been a strange awakening, not only the door business but other things as well. Flutters in my gut which could bode good or ill. A raciness to my heartbeat. The best recent awakenings, the ones that were really dawnlike, promised new beginnings, fresh starts, etc., etc., were after the birth of each child when the nurse would bring me the tiny bundles and pull the curtain around us. I was so eager to see them again and never tired of staring into their faces, even though I worried about their looks and inspected them callously.

They held on to my bra strap as they nursed, one small finger hooked tight in. In those first few mornings of their lives, the mothering juices were running strong, wrung out by a contracting uterus, and the postpartum blues had not yet set in. The hormonal underpinnings have since deserted me and I've been on my own for a while. Except for my imaginary M.D., whom I drag out like a Greek chorus to tell me how I'm doing.

"Doctor, I can't cope with my life."

"That's bad."

"Or rather I can cope for short periods of time."

"That's good."

"But I can't always be good-natured about it."

"That's bad."

"Or rather I can be good-natured about it."

"That's good."

"But then I don't like myself."

"That's bad."

"You see, I really can cope, but it makes me mad."

"That's bad."

"But nobody knows this except you and I."

"That's good."

"And my children may suspect it."

"That's bad."

I am the only one who knows I'm not doing well and I know it only at a remote level that ninety percent of the time has no bearing on my daily life. My children suspect I'm not doing well but they feel it as a vague uneasiness (or easiness since by now it's time-worn information). They look at me knowingly when they're feeling very macho and don't need my mothering. I'm doing much better than before I went to the mystic. The mystic has certainly given me something to go on, a peg to hang it on, as they say in the advertising world. But if you asked the children, they would not say "Much better"; they would say, "Terrible. She's doing terrible."

They have nothing to base that on. It's just a natural antagonism that suits them and is absolutely comfortable. It doesn't shock them either, or myself, that they should say, "Mother is doing terrible." Andrew would say, "Mother is not doing better, she's doing worse." And when he'd say it, Nicholas and Amanda would giggle nervously. That is, if they were in a good mood. If they were in a bad mood, they'd just say, "Terrible," sullenly without looking up. And if you asked them to repeat the answer, they would say, "Terrible. I said terrible. Can't you hear? Are you deaf?" and go back to what they were doing or watching and put the fingers back in their mouths or pick their noses absently, but look around before eating the contents because by now they're inhibited from doing that.

I asked a mother at the playground the other day how she began her day and she told me that her middle child, a beautiful little girl, comes in, and she feigns sleep until the child goes away.

"Why do you pretend to be asleep?" I asked, taking the role of a childless stranger who would be puzzled by a mother who daily tricked a three-year-old.

"Because," she answered without guilt, "she assaults me and I like to begin my day a little more gradually."

How knowing, I thought, and how necessary. Perhaps that's what I need to learn. Not to catapult myself into daily life like Evel Knievel plunging into his latest abyss, but instead to ease into it. Slink into the day bit by bit, acknowledging a child here, a husband there, a leaky dishwasher here, a stubborn wine stain there, my soul, my weight, my quiche, the jottings on my calendar.

Nobody can be expected to face all that without getting the cold clammies, and certainly this is neither the year nor the season to railroad myself into an emotional upheaval. My children are too little and I'm too young. I'll save all that for my forties, or my fifties. Or for his first affair. Or mine.

But maybe I'm hedging my bets because I know they would not long put up with an emotional upheaval. If all the world is indeed a stage and I am simply doing my *bit*, how long would they give me to look for myself before shrieking, "The hook! The hook!" like a bored vaudeville audience impatient to get a bum act off the stage?

How long would it take them to notice that I was shirking my emotional and physical responsibilities? That I wasn't making them eat their vegetables? Not lovingly or casually folding their socks together and putting them neatly in the drawer? They would come every morning to my side of the bed and complain to my hidden bulk that they had no socks, but would they sniff out the truth or simply follow my pointing finger to the laundry room?

What would they notice first? That I didn't care if they got fresh air? If they took their vitamins? That there was chronically never enough milk for breakfast? That they had eaten hot dogs three days in a row? What would he notice first? That we hadn't made love three days or three weeks in a row? That I hadn't cleaned the lint from the dryer, or the grease from the filter in the indoor barbecue, or the dust from the coils of the frost-free refrigerator? That the ring in the toilet bowl was no longer a ring but the whole toilet bowl? That the ring around his collar was not a ring at all but a millstone— me, the crazy wife? What if I let things go and get out of hand? What if I let myself go and get out of hand? I think that if I try to test their love by how long they will let me rest in bed, or how long they will suffer a lack of strict attention, or how long they will muddle through with socks that don't match, shirts that aren't picked up from the laundry, Sunday dinners without a proper main dish, Saturday nights without planned sociability, I will be sorely disappointed, because nobody wants to notice an almost crazy woman or an almost sick woman. They will only make allowances for a totally and dangerously sick woman and then only at the last minute and with many "pleases" that they had no idea that anyone was so sick and it didn't look that bad to them. She had been all right just a moment ago.

I am not dangerously sick and not dangerously crazy but at times I wish I were, which is almost the same. I have a "dangerously sick and crazy" wish, which is much worse than an outright death wish and must have something to do with enjoying the despair of my near and dear ones right now, close at hand, and not later from another plane of life.

And that's just the point. Why should I even be thinking about the despair of those near and dear to me? Why should I not be concentrating solely on their joy, their growth, their positive unfolding. When everything is done and we are ready to begin just living, a strange itch runs through my body. My blood itches. I want a little excitement. What is it? The snowballing effect of accumulated repetition? My own instinct for survival? My threshold of boredom? Isn't there enough here to hold my interest or is it all too much for my slim shoulders? Is mother really a madwoman or the only sane voice in an insane world?

But perhaps we're looking at it from a very narrow point of view. Perhaps destruction is the first step in creation. After all, who has really seen the whole thing from inside the womb? Who knows what little bombs burst in air before the multiplication of cells begins. There might be a little search and destroy mission, a little explosion. The heralding of a new consciousness. If there's nothing cataclysmic going on, there should be. Maybe we have to turn our values inside out. I don't feel violent or mean or bad. I feel myself and I tend to think that the neuroticism I blame myself for creating may be just so many building blocks to growth. Or maybe they are stumbling blocks to growth and maybe mother is rotten.

There are sounds from the kitchen. Benign sounds. Electric sounds. The blender purring, whipping up their orange juice and vitamin concoctions. The timer ringing for the oatmeal, the toaster being pushed and popping. It's time to get up. If I get up right this minute, I'll have time to make Andrew a balanced lunch for school instead of giving him fifty-five cents for the subsidized lunch, which includes white bleached bread, potato chips, and chocolate drink which he prefers but which leave him with a distorted metabolism when he returns home and not in the mood for talks with mother.

I feel better. I'll make my calls when things quiet down. I know D. will be after me this morning and I'll be ready for him. Some subtle chemical coupling will turn me around. An enzyme, a spurt of cortisone, a quick and efficient emission from my myriad mysterious bodily workings will set me down safely from this flight of fancy. By nine, all things will be possible. Business as usual.

Chapter Two

7:24 BY THE ELECTRIC CLOCK on the G.E. oven, a very special clock that starts my dinner when I'm out, turns my dinner off before it burns, cleans my oven while I sleep, ticks away the hours until Daddy comes home and occasionally reminds me how fast life is going by or how slow.

I'm always glad to see D. in the morning and still get a slight kick in my gut when I just reach the kitchen and anticipate seeing his face. I suspect it's the feeling of being acknowledged. One good human acknowledging my existence. I'm alive. I'm here. He sees me and smiles in recognition. It must be so. The whole world can't love you, so one person fills the need and that's why we marry. The cosmos comes to me through the love of one.

He looks up and asks, "Any headache this morning?"

Behind the calmness there is anxiety and it's not my imagination. His eyes have a pleading quality, and who can blame him? If your dearest and nearest is constantly on the verge of a debilitating headache, there should certainly be some pleading in your eyes, anxiety in your voice and a hope in your heart that those headaches should cease and desist so they don't hang down over everyone's head, hovering like malicious marsupials waiting for an unguarded moment and then pouncing crazily down on him, the boys, the baby girl.

"No." I say airily. "No headache."

No headache, everyone sighs with relief. Big headache. A rrrrrealllly big one. Everyone plows down into his bowl of Alpen. Except today it's oatmeal.

Ah mood, mood. Everything is mood in life. Or low blood sugar. The unbridled id is no longer *número uno* on life's list of culprits. It's been bumped by low blood sugar.

Monday through Friday, we all eat Alpen or oatmeal with wheat germ and bananas, except the children have been using less and less wheat germ until now I can count the grains, but I've just let it go. On Saturdays and Sundays I make everyone pancakes or, lately, waffles on an antique waffle iron I bought for two dollars at an otherwise dull garage sale (lots of plastic vases, tiered candy dishes and travel valets, one with the card still in the box, "Have a lovely trip. Love, Aunt May"). The waffles got hopelessly stuck until, to everyone's relief, I bought a can of Pam and sprayed the iron thoroughly (another two dollars).

I don't usually buy things in aerosol cans because, as everyone knows by now, parts of them don't ever disintegrate but will clutter the universe forever. Also, every can sold is money in the pocket of Robert Abplanalp, holder of the aerosol valve patent and friend and benefactor of Richard Nixon. If he wished to be my benefactor, as well, I would not be up to refusing nor would I bring up his past lapses in taste.

Rigidity is not for me and I consider it an exercise in virtue to buy things occasionally that are neither healthy or morally or ecologically sound simply because it's better to add one aerosol can to the heap than risk rigor mortis of the spirit and become so self-righteous that small vertical lines will mar my otherwise generous mouth. It is not my aim to become a grievance collector, although my near and dear ones would scoff at this statement.

Aside from these small, necessary lapses, I am stupefyingly concerned with what goes into our stomachs. Looking out at the wilderness, our house in the woods, everything *au naturel*, I think perhaps I should follow suit. Turn our backs on Orlon, Dacron, Antron, Formica, polyethylene, Naugahyde. Turn up our noses at Styrofoam, Cadillacs, intercoms, motorized beds and bars, landscaping, coordinated bed and bath. Say toodle-oo to T-bone steaks, Hamburger Helper, Cool Whip, Cup-a-Soup, Cheez-Whiz, Jell-O and Mallomars. Mutter ta-ta to Virginia Slims and the Marlboro Man. Stop giving our colds to Contac and give them instead to Vitamin C and meditation. Thumb our noses at General Foods, General Motors, General Mills, General Haig. After all, haven't they been the prime promoters of The Dream? The same American Dream that has turned into a rotten stage mother that makes sullen, greedy brats of us all? I'll leave my food dollar with Live and Let Live (a health food store, what else?).

•

My husband is always completely dressed for breakfast, even on weekends, and I am not. It is an orderliness that carries through into every area of his life—his thinking, his movements, his work. D. works for himself and could work at home except he believes it would be his undoing. His work is based on a certain precision that is missing in this house. He enjoys going to his orderly office where he has worked things out exactly to his liking, and the personal efficiency gives him pleasure. He likes clothes that fit precisely, tea carts that slip snugly into alcoves, the Water Pik in the Water Pik cubby.

D. is an illustrator. He depicts things realistically, photographically, in fact. Anyone who sees one of D.'s renderings reproduced almost always, at first glance, refuses to believe it's a painting. D. is a photographer of things that are yet to be, so to speak. Ships that haven't been built, buildings that are still ideas, oil rigs that are merely lines on paper. He is a perpetual and enthusiastic student of how things really look— objects and their shadows. Everything has a shadow and D. knows them all, how long they should be, how fat, their angles, at what point they will be intercepted by other shadows. He knows how sunlight filters down through leaves, which leaves it will touch, which it will miss. He is intimate with the reality of life, committing to memory minutiae that escape the rest of us. All this hobnobbing with reality has made D. a master of logic and deductive reasoning, but it has not, as you might imagine, given him an edge with the rest of his life, or with people. He is not so expert or at ease with people. It takes a while for him to figure things out.

His father was a painting contractor and painted houses and buildings for a living. The stunning relationship has not been lost on D. From time to time he will say, "My father painted with a big brush, I paint with a little brush." Other than that, he hasn't done much with this information. What can you do with it?

An economics professor in college had said, "Make yourself scarce in what you do and you'll make money." D. took the advice to heart. He is a licensed but nonpracticing architect, preferring to have more control of his time, his life and his source of money. This addiction to literalness has worked well for D. It has worked for him, for instance, in the stock market. He is not swayed by good news, bad news, ups or downs but plays out his plan to the end.

There is calm good humor at breakfast this morning and I'm grateful. It's tricky to get them all in a good mood. Andrew is telling the jokes and riddles that he's beginning to bring home from school.

"What did the porcupine say to the cactus?" he asks his father.

"What?"

"Is that you, mother?"

"What did the porcupine say to the cactus?" asks Nick, who repeats everything.

"What?" I ask.

"Is dinner ready?"

"Niiiiick!" screams Andrew. "That's all wrong."

"Well, in a way it's right," I say.

"What did the porcupine say to the cactus? What did the

porcupine say to the cactus?" asks Amanda, the baby, who says everything twice.

Nobody answers her.

"I have another joke. Wanna hear it, Dad?" They direct all conversation to their father. They adore him, they really do. They flip coins to see who sits next to him at meals, stir their milk in precisely the same way he stirs his coffee, wash their faces in the same cumbersome way, sit and watch the birds, birdbook in hand (usually upside down), the way he does.

"Why did Humpty Dumpty have a great fall?"

"Uhh, why?"

"To make up for a crummy summer." He shrieks with laughter and adds, "Get it? Great fall. Crummy summer."

"Why did Humpty Dumpty have a crummy summer?" asks Nick, but his father isn't listening and he gets down from his seat (he lost the toss today) and goes to stand at D.'s side. He wants his father's attention. Strangely, when they're hurt, they only want me. I pull thorns, retrieve broken teeth from blood-filled mouths, hold ice over head wounds. I'm cool as a cucumber when there's a nasty job to be done, yet I can't watch the slightest wobble of a chin when they're about to cry from emotional hurts. Andrew cries infrequently now and his tears squeak out—the sound of a small wounded animal. My stomach crumbles with his face; I can't bear to see him cry because I, most often, am the cause of his tears.

There is a neat quarter-moon gouge on his chin this morning. Memorabilia from yesterday's confrontation. It's a lovely chin with just one dark freckle to point up the whiteness.

"What hurts the most?" I asked him when it was over.

"My throat. From crying. It feels like it's closing up."

Every day there is something bad between us. His recklessness comes between us and makes me anxious and afraid. He ignores safety zones of human behavior and then quite charmingly, exuding innocence like an animal releasing an odor in self-protection, he will say, "What do you think? That I'm a piece of plastic, a piece of glass and you don't want to get near me because of the sharp edges?"

I am ashamed of what we fight over. Last night, after more badgering than I could withstand, I let him stay up until ten. At 9:57 he came to tell me he was bored.

"Bored! Bored!" I screamed, rising from my chair like the great horned owl, ready to pounce without mercy. "It's ten o'clock. You're supposed to be asleep, not bored. Are you crazy?" I have asked him so many times if he is crazy, he's no longer certain of the answer. "OK. OK," he said, fleeing to his room. "But you said I had three minutes." Before I calm down, while I'm chasing him, I realize there has been a kink in communication. How long does he think three minutes are? Does he know? Doesn't he know? Is he an innocent bystander or a diabolic malcontent? And who the hell cares?

Andrew tells me that our fight levels (his words) would go way down if I would yell at Nick exclusively. The way I was doing it now, he was having to bear Nick's badness *and* my yelling. Plus I was never, never carrying out my soft-voiced (Andrew's description) threats to Nick.

Now Andrew is a very good arguer; behind his repetitious and high-pitched whine there is a lot of sense. He doesn't think I listen, but I do and catch every nuance. But through my admiration for his fresh approach, there is a solid wall of boredom. I don't want to hear again how he feels, how it affects his behavior and why I should take quick steps to remedy the situation, no matter how dazzling the presentation. If things get horrendous and Andrew begins to strike out noticeably, I will have to do something, but short of that, I'm immune to articulate pleas for recognition and fair play.

Time plays tricks with me as well as him. His legs have lost their roundness and they're too long for his body. The calf is muscular and no longer round and vulnerable. Without any baby fat to define it, the crease has widened and lost its innocence. By surprise one day, I saw him as a baby again. It was as if I just remembered to see him as a baby before it was too late. I felt sad because I realized I had probably rushed him through. For a split second his fingers got stubby and his face changed, too, but it was too late. He had crossed over. Had I kissed him enough? Held him enough?

How much are you allowed to hug and kiss them? And where? And how long? Nobody has said. Their round, perfect bodies are a jackpot of touching pleasure. When they leave me, will I while away my dowager years with a silly small dog in my lap with curvature of the spine from my perpetual, absent-minded stroking?

We've been mismatched, Andrew and I, and it comes out in his dreams. He's got me down pat. The benign gorilla. The cement gorilla (rigid and unyielding). This winter/spring, he's trying to befriend the gorilla. His dreams include me *and* the gorilla, but he wants to make friends with the gorilla and I don't. I just hide. Talk about rich symbolism. He's been saying to me lately, "Look, don't be angry. Can't we be friends?"

It's all little things but they get me down and it gets me, too, when D. says, "You two at it again?" which puts us in a tight circle of viciousness while he, wisely, on the outside, leads his orderly life. I seem to be the only one who is not managing. Andrew expects grumpiness from me and doesn't let it deter him from following his innocent impulses or his detailed plan to drive me mad, whichever is at work here. For instance, now, it will not deter him from getting down a pint-size thermos from the shelf and pouring milk into it.

"Why are you doing that? You've already dirtied two milk glasses. Why are you getting the thermos down?"

"I want to use it."

"You can't. You can't use it."

"Awwwgh. You never let me do anything." It comes out a screech of annoyance and he begins to stamp his bare feet on the quarry tile floor. Slap, slap . . . overgrown feet slapping my nice, cool, brown floor. It occurs to me that our relationship is literary. The stuff of good Russian novels. The criminal and the police chief. The moth and the flame. At times, I am barely civil to him and the situation leaves us both wary so that when we meet again, after school or in the morning, it's always with our feelers out, touching each other gingerly, always ready to retreat to our comfortable roles of benign antagonists. The only problem is, I am the adult.

"You used to let me use it."

"Use what?"

"You used to let me use the thermos."

"Oh, that again. Yes, when you needed to go somewhere and needed a drink."

"I need to take a drink with me downstairs."

"OK, take it. But put it back when you're finished."

"Can I fill it with milk?"

"Yes."

"There's a big green thermos in the lower closet. Can I use that one?"

"No. The liner's broken."

"There's a small one, too."

"The top's missing."

He goes to the closet under the range where the thermos bottles are kept.

"Does it mean the liner's broken when you see metal inside?"

"Yes."

"Well, one you can see metal but there's another one with glass. Can I use that one?"

"You have one."

"I want to use the other one."

"The top's missing." I look to D. for a reading, but he is looking out the window.

"Can I put the top to this one on the other one without a top?"

"No." It comes out much louder than I intend but, once the damage is done, I say it again and again. "No. No. No!"

D. is no longer a spectator. He is rubbing his hand above

and below the waist of his Levi's, which means his stomach hurts or he believes it is about to hurt or else he's remembering, all too vividly, all the times it has hurt in the past. He would never criticize me, but he might say, as he has said before, that the yelling gets to him and his stomach rumbles all day.

I feel this is an allowable remark. Well within his rights. But the feeling of inadequacy begins to seep out of my bones. I am the yeller. Disturber of the peace. Causer of stomach rumblings. Neurotic manager. Unfit mother who must yell to get her way. The children want to keep me involved in this endless dialogue and they've become expert at it. Even the baby with her baby language and mixed-up verbs is expert at it, and it sounds cute and innocent, but it's not. Sometimes I feel that if I knew how to handle children instead of being such a child myself, I would treat them differently and they would respond in the joyous, orderly, nerve-soothing way that is natural to secure children. I don't know why I'm harboring such a thought. At which point I tried and passed sentence on myself. Perhaps (as my mother used to say about herself), I should not have had children. But there's little to be done about that now. They're here and I have to care for them as best I can. They depend on me and I couldn't leave them. Or at least that's what I've thought up to now.

•

D. is searching the woods for more rewarding activity, one hand still on his stomach. He notices everything and is constantly amused and excited by the behavior of the crows, the birds, the squirrels and an occasional raccoon or pheasant. There is a raccoon living in one of the trees outside the kitchen window and he used to see it every day and point it out to us, but no one else ever saw it. Maybe only the pure of heart can see raccoons in trees. Like the meek who are going to inherit the earth. Is he perhaps the only innocent among us?

To me, the woods in winter are simply a composition in

gray and remind me of the not-so-clever pictures in children's magazines that ask: "Can you find the raccoon, the chipmunk, the squirrel and the crow in this picture?" I never want to and deliberately turn my eyes away before I do. I would like instead to send my own contribution to *Jack and Jill*, directed to all the little girls. A picture of a model family all combed and smiling with a dog at their feet, a bird above their heads, a sampler in the background and the caption would be: "Can you find the pile of shit in this picture?"

He does not like four-letter words and says they do no one any good and how would I feel if the children said that to one of our neighbors. Very soon after he tells me that, I usually find an occasion to ask why he married me.

I always ask him "Why did you marry me?" And he always answers, "I knew you'd never bore me." I answer in kind, "I knew you'd never bore me, either." We were both wrong. We have bored each other concurrently. Maybe not boredom as we generally think of it. I haven't yet said to myself, "if he doesn't stop talking this minute, I'm going to die of boredom." But rather it has been that sometimes his presence, his vocal presence, is an intrusion on time that I wish were mine alone. I'm sure it's been the same for him. At times, when I am just a vacant lump of flesh housing boobs, uterus, viscera and bone, I use him like a wastebasket, rambling on and on about the children and how they did this and that, said this and that, played with this and that, ate this and that, moved this and that through their intestines.

Lately, however, there's much evidence that I'm leaving the scene. Tuning out. Not being there. Large bruises on my thighs and shins that I don't recall getting. Buttons misbuttoned. Strange leftovers in the refrigerator. I have suggested to him, to them, to anyone who will listen, that I may no longer be playing with a full deck. But everyone answers that if I truly weren't, I wouldn't know it.

The mystic once said, "You cannot be in one mental state and not suffer the consequences of not being in another?" I am suffering the consequences of not being in my proper mental human state. Being a refined Barbie Doll with every nuance of sensitive behavior worked out is still not my proper mental human state.

It pains me to know how competent I am. How resourceful in finding bargains. How adventuresome a seamstress. Where your mind is, so goes your life, say the savants. Where you put your attention is where you prosper. As I tot up my successes of the past ten years, I come face to face with what I am: an unacknowledged bastard rummaging through her past, confronting every beloved MGM movie with the question: "Is that you, Mommy?" just like the porcupine in Andrew's joke.

I am a Barbie Doll with three gray hairs and the hint of a diagonal wrinkle at the corner of my left eye. If I don't question my condition while I have the strength and the looks to do something about it, I will have to forever hold my peace, take the final vows, as they say in the convent where they give you two chances to bow out.

•

Shall I pinpoint when I began tuning out? It must have been early in the game; I don't suffer well. Perhaps when my first child was a few months old and suddenly I could not muster up any more excitement over his fantastic folds and creases, his long, sensitive fingers, minuscule fingernails, his smile. There must have been a morning when I sat up in bed in our small but charming estate cottage and posed the question to myself: "What is all of this? Where am I?" Pregnancy and birth were so irresistible, they made me irresistible, but now here I was back, the same old me. Not sadder and wiser, either, but bewildered, easily tired and suddenly without options.

The birth, the breast feeding, the whole bit simply ran its course and I became aware that what was in store for me as far ahead as I could see was a face-to-face confrontation, sometimes pleasant, sometimes neutral and most times agitated. So the first adjustment I made was learning how to blank out.

I know how to go through the day on automatic pilot; not shirking any responsibility—the motions are perfect—but simply not being there emotionally. The emptiness is now so familiar, I know it as well as I know my forearms or my wrists or the backs of my hands. Love is suspended, ambition, anxiety. I am shocked that I can empty myself so completely. I don't want to be touched, and that's not right. I can let go of beliefs, truths, friends, likes, dislikes and assume a whole new set of facts and attitudes without any feeling of loss or gain, like some neuter vacuum bag for whom all contents are the same, not caring what it sucks up or what it expels.

With my complete complicity, we go to bed when D.'s ready to go to bed. Eat when he's ready to eat. When D.'s ready to leave a party is when we leave. The rest of the time, the children decide when I talk, when I'm silent. When I'm agitated and when I'm serene.

There is a book, *The Moviegoer*, at the end of which the hero marries the girl and she is completely satisfied to allow him to tell her every move to make for the rest of her life. Where to stand at a party. What to do with her drink. What to say. What to do with her day. The route for every destination. It sounded terrific for my purposes and I began to ask my husband all kinds of questions.

I put the questions to him in a childish way because I don't want the responsibility of knowing anything. I want to start from scratch and have him fill me up with whatever he knows. I ask him what makes planes fly and if the sky is blue. He searches my face for a moment to see if I'm asking in fun or if I'm serious and, when he sees I really want an answer, he tells it to me in the simplest way. He knows what ball bearings are and what they do. He knows every model and make of airplane possible. His knowledge about airplanes has made me feel much better about flying. It is through him that

I've learned that planes don't fly by force or will power, but that a law keeps them up and does so with the greatest of ease.

When I learn this about something difficult like flying, I can accept other matters that are not readily understandable on faith. Also, although it took a while before the knowledge was my own, it hasn't left me or changed. It is now mine.

I used to think you could arrive at truth only by thinking and that it changed from moment to moment as the thoughts sped by. D., by telling me these things about the world every day, has changed my mind. I have turned around so completely that one day, while we were watching the National Science Test and the announcer asked if the U.S. should spend more money in training scientists or more on the arts, I immediately said science because only science was truth and everything else was conjecture. D. asked who said that and I replied that I had, just then.

I wouldn't say this to D. (it's been such a natural thing, he wouldn't understand) but I think this whole Pygmalion thing is coming back to haunt him.

If I hadn't married, on the other hand, I would have spent the rest of my life looking for someone to marry. And if I hadn't had children, I would have made the begetting of a child, by one means or another, my life's work. There was no other way for my generation and it's ridiculous to speculate that my life could have turned out any other way.

Chapter Three

8:25 BY MY 14K BULOVA on the drainboard, an engagement present from D. (mine to him was custom-made shirts, which didn't fit) that the children now argue over because they all want to wear it and it's badly scratched but still keeps excellent time.

It would be easy now, with a few swift moves, to salvage the day, my outlook certainly, and turn it around. The children have trooped to the bedroom to watch D. dress for work. I lag behind in my kitchen, my beautiful kitchen, which D. and I designed so sensitively—all hand-made tile and oak and big expanses of butcher block. D. always wanted me to have the best possible kitchen because he thinks I excel as a cook and he believes (learned from a Dale Carnegie business course way, way back) that you should praise and reward what is good and minimize the bad, which is why, even now, he isn't onto me. He still believes everything can be worked out or will believe it can be worked out when I tell him, as I will soon have to, that it is not working out.

Sudden bright sunshine has broken through the general grayness, a corny spotlight for my plight. My beautiful kitchen is a mess of smudges and spills. Runny, beaded spills along cabinet doors, big dots of dripped orange and grape juice turned solid and stubborn, dried bits of food. It's all been accumulating through the dull, gray winter ready to pounce on me this early spring day. As the kitchen goes, so goes the day. Messy kitchen, messy relationships. Untidy thinking. Jumbled communication.

Come to terms quickly with thine enemy, says Jesus (Matt. 5:25). A handy suggestion and I'll take it. It's a spring cleaning that's needed here. I'll beat D. to the punch. He will ask me before he leaves to "Do something," "Call someone." Or he might say, as he often does, "What are your plans for today?" which leaves me quivering with indignation. I'll round up four or six articulate people on my own and avoid the rebellion of doing what he asks. I'll call now while all the decision makers are still at home.

My address book lies on the butcher block, a small black loose-leaf number that I've had since my working days. It has my maiden name stamped in gold and the advertising agency where I worked as a copywriter. There are drips on it, too. A sticky book, a sticky situation. Never mind, set something in motion—call, invite, prepare, clean—and your life will unfold like a good children's story. Emote serenity and serenity will follow.

The mystic says we have to go within and imagine our own good news. That there's no such thing as luck. My God, no luck! What about the time I won a box of Hershey bars in the third grade? The time I almost drowned but was saved at the last minute by a fat, hairy stranger in Atlantic City? The many times I've skidded wildly out of control on icy winter streets and stopped safely just short of disaster? What about how I found my husband? What about finding this unbelievably terrific man living in the apartment above mine in callous, hard-to-bust New York? What about his falling in love with me? If that isn't luck, my God, the sky isn't blue.

Of course, the mystic's right. There is no luck. We set up our triumphs as well as our defeats. If I could believe that a simple little dinner party could be a triumph now, courage well placed. But to me, right now, it's a defeat.

Well, forget the luck, let's see who will break bread with

us and break this vicious circle of ennui. The Kennerlys? He's in stocks and bonds. She's a teacher. She talks about marriage as if it were a vaccination. Her first one didn't take. The second one (to Tom Kennerly) did. Her sister's first one had taken (but he died) and the second one hadn't but the husband didn't know it yet. The Kennerlys are a good choice. A family situation that is taking. But the line is busy.

My second choice is the Roses. He publishes trade magazines for the frozen food business. She's into Planned Parenthood. She answers the phone on the first ring. (Why are socially aware people almost always hyperactive?)

"Could you and Dave come to dinner this Saturday? I know it's awfully late to call but I . . ."

"We can't (insignificant pause), but can you make something for Food Day next Monday? It can't have meat in it but it should taste like it has meat in it. Or better. And it has to have all of the amino acids . . . like it can't have just soybeans unless it has millet or rice or whatever fills in where the soybeans are wanting, you know what I mean? Do you have an amino acids chart? There are twenty-two, I think. Go to the library. I have to run, the bus is here. Talk to you. Bye."

I am awhirl with resolve not to make a meatless wonder for Food Day when the phone rings and startles me.

"Hi, it's me." The voice belongs to my friend, Libby, whom I now remember with unreasonable happiness as a forgotten asset. "I saw a movie last night in which the mother goes crazy," she announces cheerfully. "She had three kids just like you do."

"Did they take her away?" Since the day we finally got together, Libby and I have had one continuous conversation which we pick up as though uninterrupted.

"Yep. It had to be a movie. In real life, you have to be in labor or have a bleeding head wound before they pry you loose from the vacuum." Libby and I bat around our boredom, our bewilderment, like gifted stand-up comics. We're always on the lookout for answers even though we don't fully understand the question.

"How did she look when she was going crazy? How could they tell? Was her hair a mess? Was she fat?"

"Hair a mess, yes. Fat, no. Sorry, cookie, it's not you. But she did look quite terrible, considering it was the movies. And her kids were very upset. They couldn't stand seeing her suffer."

"That's a lie."

"I don't think so. Kids want to protect their mother from suffering . . . if it's something they can see—crying or blood. Anyway the husband in the movie was a real creep and I think that helped her along. It's easy to go crazy if your husband is a real creep. But if he's a closet creep and zinging you here and there without your knowing it, then it must take a little longer."

"Did she get well?"

"Yeah, they told her, 'nice try, kid.' No, I'm kidding but she did come back and the sad part was nothing had changed. It was just as before." I'm entertaining a very foolish picture now of Libby and me alone, pooling our resources and our kids, a fine menage à sept. We're wearing long black stockings and corduroy jumpers and living somewhere in New York, poor but at peace with ourselves . . . the women. I want to rub the picture out immediately. Imagining anything vividly begins a process that eventually brings the thing to pass and I don't want to wrench poor Libby away from her nice lawyer husband, her true center hall Colonial, her Tennis Club with a paid-up membership that's just begun. What amazes me is that we both have accepted without hesitation that one of our number has every right to go crazy and we think it's sad that she gets well and has to go back.

"How are the kids?" I don't want to dissipate my thoughts. The time for running away with my girlfriend is long past. I am a woman now.

"Joshua has taken whining to new heights."

"He can't hold a candle to my Amanda. At her worst, she's worse than the worst woman you know."

"I know just what you mean. The boys, too," she adds smugly, "when they're in that mood, they're worse than the worst man you know."

"All the same, I love her. Every bitchy, complicated inch of her." There are crummy motives behind this statement since Libby has two boys and wished very much the last time for a girl.

"Please don't call her bitchy," she says seriously. "There's a woman who lives near me and she has this habit of calling her child a bitch. It's grotesque. I can't explain it to you but every time I hear her do that the image pops to mind of a hole getting deeper and deeper and this poor, unsuspecting little girl sinking lower and lower into the ground. We none of us start out being bitches."

I am comforted by her need to protect Amanda and me. She has chosen to take it very seriously. The way it should be taken.

"Can I leave Joshua with you while he naps and we can talk a little when I pick him up? I want to play tennis and the sitter can't come."

"Sure. What time?"

"About quarter to one." Things could be quite different by one, or it could be the same (D. knows nothing). But still Nick will not be pleased to see Joshua on our doorstep. He is harboring a grudge because Joshua refused to say goodbye to him three months ago. Children remember slights like that far too long. Nick, for instance, will be taking a bath and showing me how he swims and all of a sudden sit bolt upright and say soberly, almost to himself, "Joshua didn't say goodbye to me, that nitwit."

"OK." I hang up and make my way to the bedroom, momentarily distracted from my desmudging-mood-altering mission.

Our friendship, Libby's and mine, frightens us. Or rather it no longer frightens me and still frightens her. She has always thought of me as the more reckless of the two, attributing her own timidity (her assessment, not mine) to a too proper upbringing—Smith, the right summer camps, riding lessons, etc., etc. In the old days, we said terrible things to each other. We pointed out terrible things about our children to each other in moments of anger. During the worst time, when I began collecting my coat and handbag, she said, "Oh, God, are you going to leave in a huff?" Not to be outdone, I said, "Of course not." But in my head I knew I'd never come back.

The first time we saw each other again it was very uncomfortable and we pretended the children wanted to see each other. It got better than ever after that and now she's frightened because we've covered a lot of ground and overcome a lot of obstacles.

"You're the only person I can talk to," I'll say.

And she'll answer. "Please don't say that. That's the kind of thing people say when they never see each other again."

Libby reviews movies for a small local radio station. When she first got the job, she was very excited and you could see it was a transformation. To some extent she left me behind and moved to a new plateau. Now she's accustomed to hearing herself on the air and gets mad because they don't pay her enough.

"Why don't you go to New York and really make a stab at it?" I ask.

"I'm afraid. Suppose I leave the kids alone all day and make them do without me and then find out that the other thing is just so much bullshit and the only thing that really means anything is the children. Suppose I find that?" She challenges me, hands on hips.

A couple of years ago, I would have said, "Yes, you're right. Suppose the children *are* all there is." But now I know better. The children are not all there is.

Once when she was lounging on her patio listening to her own pretaped review on a transistor radio propped between her knees, she pointed to it and said, "See that. Barry thinks symbolically and literally this is what I'm giving birth to. If it was up to him, we'd have a dozen kids and I'd bake bread all day. But now, this thing held tightly between my knees has come between us. I don't even know why I hold it like this except that it feels very natural. I think the thing that disturbs him most is that I've given birth to something on my own. Self-impregnation. The ultimate threat to the male."

Libby is very precise and analytical, overqualified really to fix her deadly aim on such petty stuff. But no amount of inner hunger, unruly appetites, etc., could budge her from her nest. By her own admission, she has been psyched out beyond redemption by her mother. And will remain a proper lady to the end. She worries about her hips, the size of her hips, her ears, (one sticks out a little), if she should have another child. Her continuing innocence of her own make-up and the direction in which she is hurtling is staggering. Or perhaps it's just that we see others' lives more clearly and she sees me hurtling. It's exciting really, to see us both, all women now, as sleek objects hurtling in space.

What she has said about self-impregnation brings another conversation back into my head. Sitting on a bench in a park in Greenwich Village. A neat, slack-clad girl with her hair in a pony tail, a pale pink, ladylike lipstick on her mouth and she is saying to a friend, "So I said to him, if you're going to just rub me with one finger for ten minutes and then stick it in, we'd better turn this thing around right here. I can do that for myself. What do I need you for?"

Shattering. Not her honesty and simplicity, which was grand enough for the early sixties, but the reduction of the whole man/woman business to one very explicit sentence. Take away the picket fence, the anniversary waltz, the economic structure, the social pressures and all you're left with is: What can you do for me that I can't do better by myself?

Libby and I met when she rented one of the waterfront houses in our community for the summer. She says now that I never answered her when she spoke to me that summer and it made her feel small and embarrassed, but at the same time challenged to get some response. She would ask me questions in passing or when we were standing a few feet from each other at the water's edge. How old was my son? (We each had one child at the time.) Which house was mine? Was it going to rain? The less I spoke, the sillier the questions became. Then, one day, I answered her at length and she was absurdly happy. Of course, that was the year her teaching contract was not renewed and her spirits and morale were low. She was set up to feel rejected. Her fortunes changed quickly after that and now I'm low man on the pole. I listen to her describe me as I was that summer with the same insatiable interest that consumes Andrew when I tell him about the day he was born. It's as if she's describing another person. A person who interests me very much and whom I would like to know. Now, for me not to answer anyone would be unthinkable.

I am hell-bent on being nice. Too nice to ask the doctor who said I wasn't pregnant with Amanda why he couldn't recognize a pregnant uterus after practicing twenty years. ("My dear, I don't believe you are pregnant. You see, the pregnant uterus has a purplish tinge at the cervix and it's spongy and enlarged. But that could also mean you are about to get your period. So, go home like a good girl, and you'll probably get your period in a day or two.") But Doctor, I throw up every day and fall asleep at the dinner table. The last is mumbled inside my head since I don't have the courage to question the least medical person. Or anyone else.

I don't rebuke the grocery clerk who misprices my goods and often short-changes me as well. Nor the butcher who sneers that all liver is frozen when I ask for fresh liver. Nor the teacher who humiliates my child because he doesn't conform to questionable standards. Dear Mrs. Shroeder, please don't humiliate my child unnecessarily. When you asked the children what they did for Mother's Day, he said, in his uncomplicated, childish way, "I didn't do anything." But when he got your message—that you were going to use this information as a weapon and write it in huge block letters on a large pad, for all to see, and have it say next to his name: DIDN'T DO ANYTHING—he begged you to forget it. Were those other glib answers so important to you?

I fed the cat.

Cleaned the basement.

Helped my mother pack (That was a strange one; was mother leaving on Mother's Day?)

Took the dog for a walk.

DIDN'T DO ANYTHING.

Etc., etc., etc.

The other morning, just barely after dawn, that same child said to me, "Do you know that yesterday, today was tomorrow?" And on a recent balmy afternoon, while we were lying in the hammock watching birch trees swaying in a gentle breeze, he looked up at the leaves and remarked: "No matter how hard you look, you can only see one side of anything at a time." Hallmark should have such good writers, Mrs. Shroeder. (Again, all this inside my head.)

Everyone thinks I'm either neutral nice or very nice, but where does my swallowed humiliation go and where does it come out, if ever? Or is it snowballing in there, waiting for the avalanche? NICE MOTHER RUNS AMOK, TRIES TO SLAY LOVER AND SELF.

There is something else and I keep it separate because it overrides the niceness—a fear. A fear that someone—the butcher, the cleaner, the hardware store man, the pediatrician, the pediatrician's nurse (especially her)—will find out something about me that will be so totally and unforgettably unappealing that . . . that what? I don't know what. I don't know what they'll do. They won't run away. Nobody runs away anymore, not from cripples or bums or even blood.

Instead they'll become evasive or overly cheerful. They'll talk in generalities instead of particulars. I've seen it happen to others (although it has not yet happened to me), to women who talk too much or too fast or get nervous and start telling you what they had for lunch or dinner.

The shoemaker frightens me. In fact, he scares the wits out of me and, lately, I'd just as soon let a pair of shoes die a slow death in the back of the closet as face him. He never talks to me. He never even answers the children and they ask him things over and over. He lets me do all the talking and simply hands me a slip with a date and a price scribbled on it. Suppose he takes the sandal I've just handed him with one strap coming unstitched and throws it back at me. I couldn't handle such unexpected rudeness and would be in for a bad couple of days.

I'm not secretive about my fears and will admit them to anyone who will listen. If, in a group of two or three, one of the girls says she fears our icy country roads or being alone in her house overnight, and if she turns to me and says, "Aren't you afraid, too?" I answer, "Oh, yes. But then I'm afraid of everything." They'll laugh nervously and someone is sure to say impatiently, "Aw, come on. You're not afraid of everything." I am. And I'm getting more afraid the more successful I become. The better attendance I get at my dinner parties, the more achievements my children pile up (there hasn't been much yet but they're very smart; I expect a lot).

When I try to account for these unfounded (or founded) fears, the bizarre notion comes up that I'm living someone else's life and therefore all my actions must be calculated rather than natural, leaving me alternately scornful and bored or busy and engrossed with carrying this borrowed life-script out to an orderly conclusion. I'm on the fence as to whether to act well or badly, care desperately or not give a damn, put my best foot forward or pack it all in.

I have all this time on my hands, you see, to make sense of my life. I don't have to go to work and claw my way to the top. I could claw my way to the top right here, in the woods. I could create an elaborate structure—the best people, the right leisure time activities, good conversation, the pursuit of happiness for happiness' sake. No sarcasm here and none intended. It would certainly make things easier all around.

"That was Libby," I say to D. who has not heard the phone. Who, in fact, seldom hears it. He is most attentive to the data streaming in through favored senses and becomes so engrossed that the rest of the world can't easily intrude. Children, wife, guests, ringing telephones have to wait until his equipment cools off. Daily life, like a rasping doorbell, gives him little jolts, crashes into his private rapture. I used to think I needed his complete attention, but now I would not know what to do with it.

"Phone? What phone?"

"The phone rang. It was Libby. She wants me to watch Joshua for a while." It occurs to me he could ask why I don't have Libby and her husband to dinner but I know he won't. He's jealous, because in a moment of angry honesty I said that, at times (I hesitated to say all the time), I felt more comfortable with her than with him. She allows me more playing range and I am opening up more to her and closing up more to him. But men have always been jealous about women's talk. If they only knew. Women talk about their mothers, their children, their weight and the guilt they feel over all three. He's giving me long, thoughtful looks and will soon come up behind me, nuzzle his face into my neck and ask me to "do something," to "try."

"It's kind of late, don't you think, to call for Saturday?" I might as well bring it up.

"Maybe not. Everyone thinks the other fellow has something to do. Somebody will be free, you'll see. You'll be surprised."

Why am I irritated by his telling me I'll be surprised? There's too much of the "now be a good girl and do what you're told and everything will be all right." Who said he knows more about the world than I do and when it will or won't be surprising?

I take a long look at D.'s body. How together he looks. In better shape than he has ever been. Ever faithful to his jogging, D. seems to be blossoming in his forty-fourth year while I . . . I am immobilized. Unmeltable. Unspoilable. A caterer's dream. And what is she faithful to? . . . her eating, her equivocating.

"I had a dream last night," he says, sitting on the window seat and peering up at me over the dresser that separates us. Everyone in this house, except me, dreams away his terrors nightly. Cement gorillas with ovalish toes, trains that won't stop, vacuum cleaners waltzing merrily down the road. (Is that me leaving?)

This morning D. reports a dream of such complete frustration it stops me in my tracks. He was a golf pro but when he approached the ball there was no level place to stand. There were cracks in the ground that would have swallowed him up had he fallen in. He kept trying to approach the ball and hit it but it was just one frustration after another.

"How awful," I say. "Are there problems at work?"

"Oh, no. That's not it."

"Then what?"

"I can't discuss it right now." He looks at the children.

"Why are you bringing that up again?"

"I'm not. I don't want to. Just forget it. I didn't want to bring it up and I won't mention it anymore. It was just that the dream was so vivid and I've been thinking a lot about it this morning." But he has brought it up and in a way I'm relieved.

D.'s dream is as straightforward as he is. There is an undercurrent of sexual dissatisfaction that runs through our life. Not enough. Not the proper interest. Last night, for instance, I cried because D. and I don't make love enough. There is a place for tears in my life and they're not to be taken too seriously. When I'm trying to tell him something important, inevitably he turns away. Unconsciously, he will run out on the deck to see an airplane, to chase a squirrel off the bird feeder. It is an unmistakable turning away. Rich body language. I've never become used to it. So there you are, crying has its place. But last night, they were different tears, prompted, I think, by D.'s kind, unworried eyes on the pillow. They were tears over the waste, although I didn't present them as such. I said instead, "I feel guilty taking up your life this way. I feel guilty every night. I think, sometimes, I'd be better off alone."

"Instead of feeling guilty over not making love, why not just make love?" says D., ever the logician.

So simple in the abstract. So insurmountable in the particular. The average American couple has sex 8.6 times every four weeks. It used to be 6.2 times but the pill has upped it to 8.6. I'm not keeping up. My body is sluggishly dragging around a brain gone berserk with power. It isn't that I don't like my body (although there may be some of that now with the extra pounds) and cringe from sensual pleasure, out of touch. Your nerve endings are lost, my dear. Adrift in a sea of lard. If you were trim, you could view your body as a thriving enterprise—hair growing, blood coursing, cells renewing, bodily juices collecting. Each cell would make its contribution instead of lying neglected, uncalled. Soldiers without a war.

"I get this feeling at times," says D., up on his elbow, "that you'd just like to get it over with. I think to myself, she's saying 'let's just do it and get it over with.' "

I have imagined this scene so many times this past year, I can't now react to it. It's the same when you've imagined many times how it would be to kiss a person; when it happens, time *does* stand still. You're stuck in a pocket of time, feeling giddy and not in a hurry to do anything. What I have not imagined, unfortunately, is my answer. It is a tribute to D.'s patience, his sense of fair play, that he hasn't brought this up before. There's been a hell of a lot of marital gold-bricking going on here and I can't come up with a definitive reason. I could simply shrug my shoulders and say, "I don't feel like it, period." But there's more to it than that or I think there's more to it than that or I want to think there's more to it than that.

"That isn't true," I say finally, because D. is waiting for an answer.

"Well, if I'm wrong about that, I'm glad." He settles back down on his pillow and inches the rest of his body to his part of the bed. "Let me be the judge of what I should or shouldn't be getting. I'm a big boy." He stares up at the ceiling. "It helps to talk it out." I'm appalled and relieved that he doesn't question me further. That he doesn't want to know more. I could tell him a lot more.

I am not yet over the notion that I'm doing something bad to D. Doing something bad to his well-exercised, well-lubricated machine. My behavior is stunting his life. I'm doing something bad to him and to Andrew, the two sober, wise ones. The rest of us . . . the rest of us are round, unpredictable children, sometimes constructive and appealing, sometimes destructive and a burden. But still, without rhyme or reason to our game.

Unbidden, a cold, uncaring voice comes from me. Now it's my turn to sit up. "It doesn't help to talk when we can only come to certain conclusions, which are to keep on doing what we're doing basically."

"What would you suggest?" The question is rhetorical; he knows from my past history that I have nothing to suggest.

There is no answer. As far as I'm concerned, we're moving little tin symbols on a Monopoly board, plastic checkers on a checkerboard. This is not my life. It can't be. I can't take it seriously.

"You're not programmed to believe in marriage." (By default, D. still has the floor.) "Your mother and father were divorced. Your uncle was divorced. What long, continuing thing have you ever had? You didn't even have a savings account when I met you; you'd never stayed in one place very long. How many apartments had you had when I met you?"

"Four." I'm eager to feed him ammunition.

"See. I had one."

"You stayed in your parents' house too long."

"I was away at school."

He's trying to discredit me, discredit my feelings, this master of deductive reasoning. And now, he wants to wind it up and get to sleep. "We need to get out more," says D. sure, as always, of his ground. "We need to lead a more balanced life. Go to the movies. See other people. Why don't we plan something for Saturday? We're always glad afterward. Remember last fall, we had eight for dinner every Friday and everyone had a wonderful time and ate everything in sight. You do good work." He pats me, half-kiddingly trying to coax me into some enthusiasm for his plans. Suzy Knickerbocker, who is invited everywhere, has been quoted as saying that eight around a round table eating good food is the best nighttime fun there is. D. and I feel the same. We looked for a year to find the right round table, the right Tiffany look-alike lamp, the right bentwood chairs. The only thing we haven't perfected are the eight people.

Now he sits up and I lie down. Should I come in and tell him everything? There is something very wrong with me, of that I'm sure. As it happens, I'm not sure, but I can't admit it because he will try to convince me I don't have a leg to stand on. That I'm depressed for some other reason, that my daily headaches are no longer reasonable and that life is what you make it. He might be right, except for one thing. I'm not depressed. As a matter of fact, I'm kind of excited about certain things—but not the right things, so far, to help poor D.

"I can't stand living here," I say finally. "All this isolation drives me buggy. It's fine for you, but we're here alone all day. I'm sick of these goddam woods. I can't stand all these trees, there's so much debris. You don't even want to clear up the woods." This is such an undistinguished complaint—my God, not to like trees—that I'm wondering myself how many ways he will squelch me. "I want some grass. The children and I want some grass. We have all this land and we're stuck on the driveway. There's no place for us to go. Why do you make me feel that wanting grass is like wanting Communism?"

"Just the opposite. Grass is so American. It's the thing to have." Here he puts in a snide aside, "And I'm really surprised you're taken in. American business wants to make the machines to tend grass and the chemicals to make it grow, so they create an irresistible desire for grass and all these poor slobs spend their leisure time tending their lawns, which nobody ever walks on except to cut. Don't you hear anything? Didn't you hear what Jack Butler said? He wanted a maintenance-free house. They left the grass in Manhasset. The Rains, too. They left the grass *and* the pool in Westbury."

It isn't so much that I want the goddam grass or anything else I argue for, but waking up these mornings and thinking about it, I get the feeling that something's been snuck past me. We're living D.'s dream exclusively. We're living out *his* childhood dreams. When I mention this to him, he tells me he won't buy the idea. "Look around you," he says. "That table. You worked so hard on that table. The decor. Most of it is you." Men are so literal. They don't see the shadings of life.

It's a conundrum. So much of my childhood rooted in religion and now . . . still worshiping miracles, needing a mystic. Or is it something more basically human, and am I wrapping it all up in a nice sentimental package like Louis B. Mayer? Do we get fat and unwieldy in order to punish our men for no better reason than that they are available victims?

"You're not always unhappy," he sends out in the dark to my mute, still body.

"No. Nobody's always unhappy."

Well, now. Let's see what's at work here. He is content to put up with my lack of putting out (so to speak), my tears, my grotesque mismanagement of time. He's a big boy and he judges that it's OK to bear my ranting and raving, my periodic tantrums, if only I will . . . what? Provide a little balance to our lives, like the well-balanced meals I'm so firm about. If only I will provide some companionship, entertainment, intercourse with our fellow man—and not close my thighs to him altogether. We will go on camping trips, eat so many Thanksgiving turkeys, open endless Christmas presents.

And I? Should I continue to be led by this nice leader, opting for protection, devotion, concern, a chic roof over my head, and ignore this inner suspicion that there's more to me than meets the eye?

Bad. Bad. Bad. My current unrobust desires, my lack of interest in a clean and orderly home, plus my certainty that I'll crash the car from stretching my neck to inspect the manicured order that seems to prevail. I am mesmerized by clipped lawns, orderly flower beds, precisely stacked firewood. Order haunts me and makes me so nostalgic I'm tempted to believe that in another life I was the Queen of Cleanliness and Finesse, or maybe it's all those Ty-D-bol commercials digging into my brain.

Should I sleep with a man if I don't want to, to fulfill my sexual obligations? How will I know when I want to if I always feel I should? If I got a job and became successful on my own would I still want to? If I were thin and in love with my body would I still want to? If I tried it with a woman, would I want that instead? Is it not Dressy Bessie behind this Estée Lauder Bronzing Gel, but really Dapper Dan?

All of our arguments are the same argument and, now, so boring that sometimes we don't show up ourselves. We send our understudies. There are certain objects in our life that act as props. We go to them like pilgrims and transfer our anger, our feelings of powerlessness in changing the other, in changing ourselves, in getting life to speed up or slow down or do whatever it needs to do to help us out.

He buys clothes that he never wears. I buy wretched objects that need refurbishing. I stand at his closet and say: "Look at all this stuff in here you've never worn. You're always buying things you never wear."

"I know," he will answer innocently.

When it's his turn, he seeks out the junk I bring home with unrealistic hopes for its renewal. Fiddling with the radio dial one Sunday morning, I heard a lady evangelist say, "Don't entertain doubt as if it were a favored guest. Boot it out and say, there's no place for you here." I entertain false hope as if it were a favored guest, except I don't see it right away.

A good example is the child's worktable facing me. I suspect it isn't a real antique since I have four others just like it and just as wobbly, which I purchased on a day when, huge with child, I went looking for odds and ends at a sale of the contents of a home. There was a hand-lettered sign propped among them saying . . . so many ways to use them. Yes, yes, I thought, and took all five, stuffing three into my car and returning the next morning for the remaining two.

The past, the past, I seem to love the past. But I couldn't bear it if some Central Park West shrink told me it was simply crude symbolism. Just some two-bit pun from my subconscious (not really a pun, of course, since the subconscious knows no humor).

D. insists that communication is important, but our lines have been written and the script is all worked out. We'll talk on and on about the last most devastating subject on a scale of ten. It could be sex. It could be money. Or how I dominate the conversation on an evening out.

Whatever we talk about is simply a smoke screen for the real issue, which is—what is to become of us if we continue on this suffocating path, giving our pleasant dinner parties, taking our winter vacations? What will we end up with—a distinguished him and a humdrum me?

"So will you try?" he always ends it, leading me back like

an overly excited child to the familiar world of reason, hot subsidized lunches, traffic lights and such.

I think I'm missing the point entirely but I know there's a point to be made. My accumulated complaining lies like a lump in my throat and crying it out won't do the trick anymore. I have to say the words. Ask the big questions. Am I trapped because of the children or did I bear the children to create a trap? I fear his anger. He'll be angry at first, there's no avoiding that. Then what? Will I end up comforting him? Will I have to have machismo in this brave new world? What's machismo?

Daily, I convince myself (way down beneath the easy manner and Room Mother confidence) that the life I lead has meaning and a higher universal purpose. That the children crying for an absent Daddy or Mommy would truly be sad. I'm projecting for my children with Vaughn Monroe and Perry Como emotions. Who knows what one will shed tears for in the next century. Or if tears and sadness will fit into the picture at all.

"Please don't be angry with me, I can't stand it." That's the way I end the worst rifts. They're not the right words, or truly felt, but they do. I'm chagrined that everybody in the house, big and little, is taken in by the clumsiest conciliatory gesture on my part. Maybe they love me or feel sorry for me. What I could not stand, up to now, is to take my anger, frustration, whatever, to the point where I could not turn back. I want to go as far as I can without losing everything, but it's a dangerous game and tiring.

Chapter Four

10:14 BY THE CAR CLOCK, chronically but dependably five minutes slow. A clock that urges us to step on the gas or let up depending on whether we're out to kill time and calm restless spirits or really going somewhere and already late.

We drive everywhere here; there's no other way. And the car is good to us, too, giving us new spirit and life when we've tired of each other or our house. We're off to the playground now with perhaps a short stop at the supermarket. I will resume my telephoning when the children nap. With children you've got to keep moving; their needs carry you along. If I were alone, I'd change things more often, my life. But with them, they need to have their routine—the playground, their lunch, their books read to them, their shots.

Nothing's resolved about the dinner party business. I want to be sure we're not overlooking a really hot prospect. D. and I were distracted at the end. As he was leaving, Nick started in with the jumbo jet business and D., so patient, let him talk it out. Nick doesn't like being left behind in the mornings (nor do I), so he usually wheedles some promise from D. to hold his imagination until evening. Today he asked for a ride on a jumbo jet and D. (unwisely) said OK. Sometime. He's been asking me every five minutes if it's time to go on the jumbo jet. I have to remind D. not to agree to these things. Nick can't handle it.

Driving wasn't always easy for me, although now I hardly think about it. When D. and I moved from the city he bought me a foreign car with a conventional gear shift and I couldn't learn to drive it. Eight months pregnant, I waddled off to the Rhodes Driving School where they gave me over to a heavy-set man with an unhealthy pallor who chain-smoked his way through my lessons. He told me this was not his regular line of work. And what was his business? Giftwares. He dabbled in Zippo lighters, small gilt-framed paintings done on velvet, shellacked tree chips with the message, "Home Is Where the Heart Is." He tried to interest me in the velvet paintings. I wanted simply to learn to drive and have my baby, but I was in no position to reject anyone here in the wilds, beyond suburbia, beyond public transportation. My condition made me timid, eager for protection, and I needed his protection to keep me from killing myself and my baby in the car.

The chain smoker spoke often of my imminent delivery as the time I would "drop it." "You're not going to drop it on me, honey, are you?" he wheezed each time he swung into the passenger seat and I squeezed myself behind the wheel. *My* baby, dropped like a handkerchief, a ball, a gum wrapper? Was I littering the universe?

I stuck with the giftwares salesman because I was afraid to tell him I didn't wish to continue. That I didn't like him, his pallor, his conversation or his hand on my edema-filled knee. I was also afraid to tell him I didn't want his paintings and made D. the culprit.

"My husband chooses everything we buy," I said. No lie here, either. D. did choose everything. His training, his heightened sensibilities over his space—the air quality, the view, the noise level—made him more qualified to decide what should surround us.

"You're going to be living with it a long, long time," D. would say each time I expressed a preference for something— towels, sheets, dishes.

In the beginning of our marriage he brought home many

Luxo lamps, the metal lamps that clamp to a surface and swivel, go up and down, placing light exactly where it's needed. The fifth one he brought home made me cry, which confused D. But over the years of constant conditioning, I've grown to agree with him. Luxo lamps *are* superior to almost any other kind of lamp for giving light, which is what a lamp is supposed to do.

When my eight driving lessons were up, I forgot about driving and had my baby. Then, when it was time again to get behind the wheel, I realized that I was more frightened than ever and decided to visit Albert Ellis, the sex psychologist, and get some counseling. We had worked out things before, Albert Ellis and I; his routine suited me fine. The session lasts half an hour and he's not interested in many return visits. He gets quickly to the point and, although every other word out of his mouth is "fuck," in a way, it puts you at ease.

"What the fuck are you afraid of?" he asked.

"That I'll crash and kill myself."

"And?"

"And I'll die."

"So?"

I thought a minute. His stocking feet peeped out over the footrest of his Barca Lounger. He was flipping index cards as he spoke. Was he rehearsing a speech on my time? After all, he was a sex expert. No timid housewife afraid of a stick shift (phallic though that was) needed *all* of his attention. A child molester, maybe, but not me.

"So?" he prodded. "What's so terrible about dying?"

"So. I don't want to have a fucking crash and die," I replied, ever the follower.

"Why do you want to give yourself a pain in the ass about driving?"

"I don't."

"You do or you wouldn't be having such a fucking bad time. It's obviously unfortunate to die, but if you keep obsessing about how *awful* it is, and how you *must* not die, you won't be able to concentrate on how to live—and how to drive well!"

"What are you talking about. I . . . ."

He ignored my obtuseness. "Look, the point is driving a car is not that goddamned hard—if you focus on *it*, and not on what a shit you would be if you drove poorly and got yourself killed."

I had nothing left to say. What was there to say? I thanked him and left, feeling mysteriously relieved. Only twenty minutes of my half-hour had been used up and I had a twinge of regret but felt silly bringing it up. After that day, I began to drive regularly and had no more thoughts of crashing.

Perhaps it was time to see Albert Ellis again. And how would the conversation go this time?

"Do you remember I came to you about driving?"

"No."

"Well, I did and you helped me."

"Fine. What's the matter now?"

"I don't want to do anything."

"So?"

"So I have a husband and three children that want to do all the things that a normal family does. But I don't."

"What do they want you to do specifically that you don't want to do?" Groping for his index cards (which, I discovered later, had my record on one of them).

"Well, today, for instance, my husband wants me to make some effort. I think he doesn't care whether anything comes of it or not, as long as I make some effort . . . show him I'm trying."

"Trying what?"

"To fix our most immediate need . . . his need. To have some sort of social life, to join the race, as he puts it. I used to do that very well but now I don't want to do it anymore. I don't want to do anything. It's all so pointless. I would really like to be alone for a long, long time."

"What's stopping you?"

"My children are small . . . I couldn't just leave them. And my husband . . . it isn't as if . . . I couldn't."

"Why not?"

"I'd feel guilty. Terriby guilty. What good would it do me to be alone and feeling guilty all the time?"

"Why would you feel guilty?"

"Because I'm their mother. I'm his wife."

"But isn't that what you don't want? To be their mother and to be his wife? You want to be yourself."

"Yes," I say, my face brightening. "That's exactly it. In fact, I think I *should* leave. That it's weak and slovenly to stay."

"So why don't you go?"

"I'm afraid."

"Of what?"

"That it will be worse out there. That I'll be lonely."

"What's so terrible about being lonely? Loneliness usually means aloneness plus shithood—putting yourself down for being alone. If you stop downing yourself, you might enjoy being alone."

I see the trap and stop. I'm not ready for such clarity of thinking.

I do leave them sometimes, in fantasy. I awake somewhere, lying in a bed of unrumpled sheets, superwhite muslin sheets that one gets in hospitals and cheap motels. Long tunnels of time stretch out before me and I yawn lazily (very uncharacteristic in real life).

I lie perfectly still in that new, strange bed and spell out the days of my life. Then I picture strange hands soothing the children. When they ask to play aggigga, no one will know that it's a mysterious game of acrobatics known only to us. The younger boy needs to be coaxed to urinate or else it's too late. Andrew can't enter a semidark room without great anxiety. They like to race the mailman to the box. They like to put the flag up when there's a letter to be picked up. I see

Amanda's huge, dark eyes questioning another face. She eventually snuggles into another neck. I keep at it until I bring myself to tears. Cheap tears.

But after I get past the tears, theirs and mine, I start to think how it would be for me to have a whole new identity. Could I face what I was? I'd like to go out West at first, where there are long stretches of scrubby land without much interruption. A place where you can sit in a field and see the reeds waving in front of your face. The Phillips 66 sign at the gas station waves. Everything moves, favoring one side from being pushed so long by the prevailing winds. There's nothing to stop the wind from coming across the barren prairies. A truck comes every five minutes, but its noise is just part of the wind. There's so little around.

The monotony of the landscape would be perfect for my purposes. No Walden Ponds for me. I'd become a waitress at a roadside diner where the clientele was mostly passing through and work the split shift, 11 to 3 and 5 to 10, at Jersey Charlie's. "What'll it be?" I'd say, while I swiped the counter with my cloth and unclipped the pad and pencil off my apron. When people asked where I was from, I'd say, "Oh, back East. Small, dumb town." What a relief not to tell what my husband did for a living or where I went to school or how many children I had and the ages.

I'd have all my sugar bowls filled and the salt and pepper shakers and the mustard and ketchup Squeeze-Eeze bottles before the lunch crowd started in. At night, I'd go home to a small rented room furnished with maple furniture, the shellac slightly chipped. There would be a chenille bedspread, faded pink-flowered wallpaper and skimpy lace curtains over the one window that wouldn't keep out the thin morning light. Toilet and shower in the hall.

I'd do absolutely nothing to fix up the room or make it personal. No ormolu. No Chippendale. No chinoiserie. Unlike first ladies and traveling actresses who dote on their memorabilia and bring it along by the pound to comfort them, I

would take comfort in the utter impersonality of everything. No knickknacks to love or dust. No favorite framed needlepoint. My specific delight would be the impersonality of everything. Without personal associations to excite my feelings, I would begin to see things as they really are and be whatever way it came out that I was when I wasn't reacting to those around me. When I wasn't playing to the crowd.

I might or might not use expletives, since D. wouldn't be around to disapprove. I might be tough or innocent. Dumb or knowing. Easy to know or distant. Kind or indifferent. Glad to be alone or restless. But I would not be putting on my Room Mother face. Or my dinner party face. Or my playground face. Or my wife face. Or my premenstrual face. I would divest myself of feeling as I've known it and mingle with dangerous, uncomplicated people.

After a long, long time of not expecting anything and not waiting for anything to happen (especially the last, which is my chronic condition), perhaps I would begin to fill up again, but so slowly that those who saw me would think I was doing nothing at all.

What a relief not to withhold rage, hold my tongue, pretend injustices (real or imagined) away. What a relief not to say, "Good evening, dear, and how was your day? Not good? Oh, so sorry. And mine? Well, you know, mine is the same every day. Oh, no. No. I'm not complaining."

I take the children with me when I leave, at times. We arrive at a new place, a big city where for the first few weeks everything is exciting for them and for me. Andrew has never wanted to live in the city. He explains it thus: he says the country has more sun *and* more shade. More trees. More houses and fewer buildings. I think he suspects I would like him to like the city. But his father likes the country.

Sometimes, it's a quicker trip. The deli man asks after the children and why aren't they with me. "The old man is home," I reply.

"Oh, he's giving you a break, huh?"

"No, I gave him a break and that's why he's home."

Does he believe me? Am I a credible tough-tender babe who is mostly flighty and doesn't have a thought beyond, "Is the ham lean today and should I get the liverwurst that's on special even though the texture and color are alarmingly unlike anything that's ever been in the ground or on the hoof?" I would really like to ask him about the sodium nitrite and the sodium nitrate in the cold cuts and if he really believes they cause cancer in humans as well as rats or is that a bunch of shit. I would like to tell him that his Danish ham, which is perpetually on special, is much too salty and ask if he knows that after a boring life, which, according to *Prevention* magazine, is the first killer, salt is the next.

I would also like to suggest to him that he shouldn't say "Hi, Hon" to me and ask if he would say "Hi, Hon" to Indira Gandhi or Golda Meir or my husband if they showed up at his counter. Finally, I'd like to ask about the rice pudding. I've never seen anyone buy the rice pudding and I'd like to know if he makes it daily, or weekly, or monthly or yearly or what. There are so many questions to ask the deli man and that's only the beginning.

Huh. Self-deceit hovers around me like a cloud of French perfume. Me, living a quiet orderly life, thinking quiet orderly thoughts? If I left I would duplicate my present life to the letter, only it would be my old boss Benton calling the shots. Mark Van Doren says we're all suckers for things the way they are so it's foolish to think I would turn into a contemplative, well-ordered woman. I would probably try to recapture what I was before I met D.—at least the physical circumstances.

D. and I met when we were both fully mature, I in my late twenties, he in his early thirties. If the truth were stretched, he could be the boy next door (he was actually the man upstairs), living in the apartment above mine when I moved uptown from the Village to a brownstone across from the

Jewish Museum. I had tired of the Village and its lopsided constituency, the high-strung people, the high-strung dogs. My next-door neighbor had been a dwarf. Every few years, I will say to D., "Do you know I used to live next door to a wonderful dwarf?" And he always answers, "No. But if you hum a few bars, I'll fake it."

I marveled that this tiny creature—who daily was stared at, pitied, avoided, shoved, run away from, stooped down to, smothered, twice a day amidst a forest of legs and bulging thighs in subways, who had to scramble up to sit on luncheonette stools, whose legs never touched the floor when she sat, who seemed like a lifelike doll with her fantastic blue eyes and silky blonde hair but with legs permanently turned inward, chubby, stunted, childlike—had the guts and stamina to get everything she had coming to her in life. (Once she went to the Little People's convention, four feet and under, and when she told me about it, it broke my heart.) She married a "normal" short man and carried a baby nine months, but just before birth, it strangled in the umbilical cord.

Her mother, a very tall woman, was thrilled when she married and gave her a proper wedding with a catered reception at an establishment that specializes in such things. At the wedding, the dwarf danced with her father, although he was very tall also, and everyone was glad when the dance was over. She has since adopted a baby and the three—mother, father and child—lead a creditable life, entertaining on a small scale (no pun intended).

How would my children react to her? Would they sense anything? "My goodness, you're so little. Didn't you eat your broccoli? Will you get bigger? Are you a Mommy or a kid?" They would ask all the questions and forget about it and have as good a time as with anyone else who crossed their path.

In my new uptown apartment, I could hear D.'s every move through his thin hemp rug from Macy's. He jogged in place before breakfast (sensible, good self-image), left each day at the same early hour even though he was self-employed

(responsible, a go-getter), came home late every night but not too late (interesting but not a debaucher).

We were always meeting in the halls, those dark, intimate, poorly lit halls. Once he became ill and I took him up a bowl of fruit: two oranges, an apple and a banana. I kept thinking of the scene in *The Outlaw* where a determined and buxom Jane Russell crawls into bed with a feverish, defenseless Jack Buetel. In the next frame, he bounces out of bed.

The first time we made love, D. said to me: "Look what I found, Ma. Can I bring her home? Can I keep her?" We were married a year later in my home town of Washington, D.C., by a minister who insisted on counseling us before the ceremony. "Marriage is a long journey," he said, "with many unexpected incidents on the way."

I always felt I got the better of the deal when we married but never let that drive me to idolatry, nor did I give him undue consideration. Some things I overdid (the dinners were colossal: Sweet and Sour Pork with Herbed Rice and Stuffed Mushrooms, Potatoes Clemenceau, Shrimp and Olive Jambalaya, Spiedini alla Romana). Some things I never got the hang of (taking his suits to the cleaners). I didn't know when his suits should go to the cleaners, his shirts to the laundry. I never ran an orderly house. The running of our lives overwhelmed me; I could not sort out the priorities. I never hung notes on the refrigerator with magnets shaped like ladybugs. I didn't maintain the bulletin board. D. still to this day urges me to make lists. "Why don't you ever make lists?" he says, ever the Daddy to me, ever the balking child. We are playing out a situation comedy, but which one? *Father Knows Best.* A satiric, transsexual *Maggie and Jiggs?* Or a pornographic psychodrama, *There's a Whip in My Valise.*

I don't want to become the list lady, itemizing my life away. I don't want to check off my chores like a storeroom clerk forever working in the bowels of the building and constantly ordering supplies, keeping strict check of his inventory. Ever up-to-date. Besides, the lists I would really like to

make would not fit into our scheme of things. I want to get rid of all my funny faces. To itemize all the life plans I'm not living and try to make a good case for mine. On the other hand, we do have to eat and I do always forget the mayo, the pickles, the Lifebuoy and a new Mister Tuffy (the old one is a shambles).

D. still hauls his shirts to the Cleanland near his office, where he stares hypnotized at the black girls who run the pressers, thump, thump, over the shirts, crunching buttons as they go. To him, their numb existence would be unendurable because he does not know how to tune life out.

In those early days, D. was glad to maintain himself. The less things changed in our lives, the less married we felt and that was comforting. He went to his job. I went to mine. We went on like that for two years. He illustrated. I wrote advertising copy for a pathetic-looking doll that said thirteen things when you pulled her chatty ring. My first test doll, Sister Baby, had said five things. Not just "mama" and "papa" but complete emotional phrases: "I'm hungry. I'm wet. Take me out. Tuck me in. Don't leave me." Not a word about love, only dependence.

To look at the commercials I wrote then is to get some inkling as to what was going on inside my head—it was a psychological grab bag. The doll I was trying to sell was calculated to arouse pity and so were the thirteen things she said. Her startled face was stuck right on her body without a neck. Her legs dangled lifelessly with just a seam, no thighs to hold them on. The commercial went like this:

> There is a living room scene with a man sitting in a big easy chair and a woman, too. Maybe another couple. A St. Bernard or some other big dog. To be shot with a fisheye lens so everything looks bigger and a bit distorted. Pan to the little girl sitting on the floor in the middle of the room. She's looking around with awe. Everything looks enormous to

her. Come in with a very soft voice-over. "When you're only four years old, the world is a mighty big place. Mommy and Daddy are a hundred feet tall. Uncle and Aunty are monstrous big, too. Rover looks like a giant bear. Daddy's reading chair is a mountain. When you're only four years old, you need something little in your world. Something that's even littler than you are." The camera pans to a corner of the room and we hear a little voice say, "Will you take care of me?" The little girl walks over and sees Poor Thing. "What a funny-looking doll," she says. "Why she's even littler than I am." "I'm just afraid of everything," says Poor Thing. "Don't worry. I'll take care of you," says the little girl. She takes the doll in her arms and rocks her. The announcer comes in. "We know there are lots of little girls like this one who want something little to take care of. So we made a lot of funny-looking dolls, we taught them thirteen funny things to say and called them all Poor Thing." Cut to the doll sitting on a shelf in the store saying, "I'm afraid of noisy boys." Then the announcer: "Tell Mommy to buy you Poor Thing today. She's the funny-looking little doll that says thirteen things. And you know she's great cause she's made by Little Critters." There's a parting shot of the doll talking on and on: "I get butterflies in my stomach. Is that thunder? Are you my friend?"

I was charting my life. The career was simply a smoke screen for my real occupation. I was after a noisy boy that I wouldn't be afraid of and who would take care of me. Announcing my intent to produce little critters that were even more frightened and in need of protection than I was. The oppressed seeking to oppress. Seemingly, all this took place in a miasma of fear, stomach flutters, timidity, but behind it all, a cool, calculating mind that knew how to produce a solid scenario.

For our own amusement—or enlightenment—we (the art director and I) created an elaborate spoof on the commercial. Where the announcer said, "Mommy and Daddy are a hundred feet tall," there were two towering apes. For monstrous big Uncle and Aunty, there were two hippopotamuses. Rover was a dinosaur. Poor Thing was a tarantula who got the little girl in a corner and ate her up.

The child inside us all still fighting the overwhelming adult world. Will I make short work of D. only to be gobbled up by my own children? It boggles the mind.

One day, as if on schedule, I said to D., "I want something alive in my life. A dog. A plant. Something." I was afraid to ask for a baby. In the sixties, you didn't tell a man you wanted to get married. (Bad.) You told him you didn't want to get married. (Good.) Telling him you wanted to marry him was like admitting you wanted him to get cancer or hit by a car. That you wanted his life to suddenly turn sour. For the same reasons, you didn't tell a husband you wanted a baby. (Bad.) You told him you didn't want a baby. (Good.)

It was a hot day and we were walking across the Triborough Bridge. We had taken a bus from our apartment and walked through Harlem giggling at the graffiti, a furniture store named SAV-U-BUX, a travel agency urging well-heeled Hispanics to *Vuele Ahora, Page Después*. Before we knew it, we had walked the entire bridge, ending up in a neighborhood park in Astoria where elderly men were playing boccie. On our way back, on the bridge, watching the traffic alongside, strangely detached from our life, I made my plea for some live thing.

D. knew instantly something was up. He is always appalled when I bring up the next step in our lives. But how else would we get on with it? Someone has to bring it up. I don't know why I wanted a baby. I hadn't been thinking or dreaming about it consciously. "There's nothing alive in our house," I said and it was true. I didn't like the way we were tiptoeing around our life. There were no bookshelves up. Nothing permanent. We had a terrace with an ailanthus tree growing on a strip of soil and I didn't even pick out the weeds. When I think what I would do with that terrace now. The vegetables, the marigolds, the jack-in-the-pulpits. We didn't know. We disdained so much in those days, but a lot must have disdained us, too.

One Sunday, a few months later, D. and I went for a drive to the North Shore of Long Island to "browse" for houses. By Thursday, we had purchased two magnificent acres a few yards from Long Island Sound. On Friday, I found out I was pregnant. Our life moves quickly, sometimes.

If my background was checkered and off-beat, certainly D.'s was normal to the extreme. He was a caddy. He had friends named Philip Engledrum and Herbie Ingham and Joe Morehead. He was pushed in a wicker carriage by his mother and she tucked groceries between his legs. He used to have tea with her; he was her tea pal and when she watered the plants, she made believe they were talking back and thanking her. His friends would come around after school and yell "Hey, Ritchee" and he would either come out (for a friend) or say nothing (for an undesirable younger brother like Frankie Dimitroff). He was invited to friends' summer houses where the eggs (to his surprise) were palatable and cooked to his liking. Now he recalls coming home and telling his mother about it and surmises it must have hurt her feelings. Am I his mother? Is he mine? In an article titled "I Want a Boy Just Like the Girl that Married Dear Old Dad," it says we all marry our mothers, men and women as well. But with so much of my childhood spent in a convent school, is he my mother or Sister Mary Josephine?

"Doctor, D. is measured, logical, prudent, whimsical, nature-loving and never holds a grudge."

"That's good."

"Doctor, I am frenetic, emotional, suspicious and easily fatigued."

"That's bad."

"Doctor, do you believe D. is all good, and I am all bad?"

"Yes. (Sorry, Mom.)"

"Doctor, you're a horse's ass."

Chapter Five

SOMETIME BETWEEN ELEVEN AND HIGH NOON.

On a scale of ten, this playground would rate a six: three swings, a slide, a merry-go-round, some monkey bars, and a discarded fire engine with four flat tires all embedded in soft, powdery, workable sand. There are green slat benches scattered around for mothers or guardians. There are one or two guardians but mostly mothers who know each other by sight if not by name.

"My Daddy is going to take me on a jet airplane," announces Nick to the first woman he sees.

"Oh, you're lucky," gushes the mother, who looks up at me and smiles, which means she wouldn't mind if I sat and talked to her. We seldom exchange names here, although we're intimate to a fault, discussing miscarriages, missed periods, lucky escapes, immaculate conceptions, marathon labors, record birth weights, preemies, awake and aware births, asleep and grateful births, nice obstetricians, sadistic obstetricians, sadistic nurses.

"Are you going away?" asks the woman.

"No. He's just saying that." I want to move on.

"Yes, I am," says Nick defiantly.

I roll my eyes at the mother and she smiles in understanding. We all behave well here—control ourselves, that is. Our voices are well-modulated, sometimes loving and interested.

Some come here, though, who have packed it in and there's no shred left. They sit and knit, barking orders mechanically while the knitting needles click viciously. They don't care what the rest of us think, which, to me, is a plus, but a sad way to come about such independence. There are all kinds. It takes all kinds, they say, but mostly middle-of-the-roaders like me, who can go either way but, mostly, I hope, the good way.

Cooing and singsong baby talk is coming from a newcomer at the swings, a young mother talking to a bored, vacantly smiling two-year-old on the middle swing. She's squatting in front of him, and with each swing he barely misses kicking her in the face.

"Whee," the mother is saying, "and upsy goes Davey. Wheee and upsey goes Davey. Ooooh Davey, he isn't having any fun at all. No fun at all." The archness is lost on Davey who has not changed his bored expression.

A slim, jean-clad woman with short blonde hair comes and sits too close to me. "That's the kind that drowns the kid in the bathtub before he's three. 'Tell me, Mrs. Schwartz, why did you kill your baby?' 'I couldn't get him to laugh. I tried everything but he wouldn't even smile.' " I nod wanly, making a big job of taking the children's shoes off. They want to play barefoot in the sand. I don't want to encourage this intense woman or be part of her sisterhood. At least not yet. It's not that I disagree with her, but I'm made uncomfortable by her well-thought-out observations. Last week, for instance, while we were all complaining in our half-hearted way about baby sitters and how young ones ate you out of house and home and old ones talked you to death, she said, "Nothing will really change in our lives until the men start taking the children to work with them." Naturally we tried to ignore it, as you would some precocious thing a child might say about sex. But she went right on. "The problem is not motherhood as much as it is fatherhood." Our heads hung down on our chests. "The role of the father is nonexistent. Supposedly, the father goes off to the corporate world to make money to support the family, to make it a better world. It's unreal yet it totally controls us. If they took the kids with them to work, the decisions would be more human. The fact that they wouldn't take them"—a snort sneer—"well . . . that's just a real hidden way of saying our work, mother's work, isn't important because you can't do important work with little kids around."

With the least encouragement, her arguable theories would tumble out and I wouldn't be able to call a halt. She must see me as a convert, sensing my soft spots, birds of a feather, etc., etc. But I'm not a feminist, that I know of. Just the same old me with the same old resentments and anxiety, which is not to say I want D. washing the dishes and dawdling down the aisles of Shop-Rite Supermarket while I trot off to work in my leather boots. D., whom I married for his craggy look, his protective chest and arms, his protective humor and reason.

But you know, D. did one thing to me that was unforgivable and I'm recalling it now, maybe through her power. Her feelings, being so strong, perhaps have touched off something in me.

One hot summer night, D. and I accepted (rather coolly) an invitation for drinks extended even more coolly by friends of friends. It was a mistake from the start, unknowns meeting to satisfy an absent third party. The four of us sat out in the garden of the strangers' summer rental house swatting mosquitoes and trying to decipher, during the gaps in the conversation (which was not flowing), the origin and purpose of some vicious-looking potted plants around us, some with just one huge blossom amid sinister, unnatural leaves.

Finally, I said to the strangers, who seemed to have a perfect life, "Who are your friends? Whom do you see for pleasure? How do you entertain? What do you like?" I wanted to know certain intimate things about their lives to salvage something from the evening, I suppose. D. says I'm always asking people if they're happy or if they know what would make them happy, or some other deep and disturbing question that startles them. My question that mosquito-ridden night did not faze Mr. and Mrs. Perfect, and they began to rattle off their friends: doctors, lawyers, and many, many advertising people. I latched on to the last and began talking about my advertising career and tried, stupidly, to find one mutual shred of similarity between their successful, party-going, unmarred, self-assured advertising executive friends and myself, just recently marred by four pregnancies, one of which became a long and macabre vigil over a fetus that seeped out of me slowly and maddeningly over a period of seven months. The D-and-C report labeled it an "ancient conception," which gave D. and me a sober few days. It's not easy (however fascinating) to witness large chunks of "something" slipping out of yourself and never know when to expect them. Every now and then, a sudden warm release between my legs. I'm not yet over the feeling that a rush of blood could begin from me at any time. A torrent escaping my mysterious equipment. All of it out of view.

On the way home that crummy evening, D. mentioned callously (quite unlike him) that things were really pathetic when I had to make conversation out of something that had happened so long ago. "Is that all you can find to talk about? Something that happened ten years ago? Hasn't anything interesting happened to you in all that time?"

Sometimes it takes a remark like that to jolt you, a startled Lazarus, out of the tomb. Now here's this slim, braless woman jolting me again. Or doing her best to.

"I hate mornings," she is saying, and you can see a vivid, hateful picture jumping to mind. "The kids have become my responsibility in the morning. My husband likes to stay up late. He does his best work late. Now I've never been a night person so I can't say he's cutting me out that way." She looks around at the women around her who have drifted together in a clump near the slide to rescue their offspring as they tumble down. She's suddenly meek—the other side of the coin. "Why does a man, the way things are and the way he goes to work, why does he want to have a family? What's in it? It must be that they're programmed and there's nothing can be done about it. But someday, like the appendix, maybe someday, we won't have it anymore. I think I only half-have it. Oh, forget it," she ends it, suddenly impatient with herself, "something is wrong with me, today."

It's catching. First her, now me. Something is wrong with me, today. Or right with me. "What's right with you?" asks Reverend Ike, whom I used to watch on the sly before it was chic to admit everything. Has all this talk of liberation finally filtered to my patch of the woods? Am I noticing things more lately or is it my age? Perhaps I've just entered the last half of my life and I want to make peace with my world.

This young woman's sudden meekness, her descent to our level of aimless questioning makes us eager to console and befriend her. We all want to tell now what we hate the most.

"I hate being fat," says a long-haired dead ringer for Ann Sheridan. Her two young daughters are fastidious replicas of their mother. Three Ann Sheridans staring out of clear hazel eyes. "It's a whole physical thing, the wear and tear on your body. Just being pregnant. And after the baby is there, it's like being immobilized. You can't just pick up and walk free. You can't even get out of the house and walk. It takes knowing a sitter. Calling a sitter. Picking up the sitter. Getting ready for the sitter, cleaning up so the sitter won't think you're a slob. It's a drain and I think a lot of us can't afford the energy so we stay home and sit. And we get fat . . . our legs get fat." We all murmur assent like a Greek chorus.

"I hate their games," I say. "I hate Cross Over The Bridge, Slippery Spoons, Tension, Trouble. I hate Trouble especially. They're all a chase. A stupid chase over absolutely nothing."

"I can't sit down and play games with them," says the first mother. "It's a fake. They know it's fake. He can do that. He's good at that. He can lower his mental level down to that, I think. I get this constant feeling that I'm missing something out in the world and, yet, I'm sure if I went out into the world, I'd feel the same way . . . that I was missing something. That's when I get the most depressed, thinking about myself and trying to figure out why I can't just put it out of my mind. Just do the job. Enjoy it and learn how to really just relax." It's funny, her choice of words. That's what men have been telling prone women for centuries: relax and enjoy it. "This should be a perfect opportunity to really get to know your kids. There's not all that much pressure on you. You should relax and build up your energies."

It's strange, what we hate. It doesn't sound like much piece by piece. It reminds me of what a reviewer said recently about a collection of prize-winning stories: chronic depression is hardly news and needs another turn of the screw to become art. The same is true of our complaining; it needs another turn of the screw to raise it into something over which we can drastically change our lives.

The mother of a small boy now chimes in. "I always thought it would be a wonderful thing to stay home. I could read a book whenever I wanted to. Secretly, I was sure I was the lazy type and it would suit me fine to just sit around reading. But I'm not happy staying home and reading a book. It brings more guilt because I still don't feel right. So I say to myself, look at what you have. I have everything I can possibly want. I can go out and buy what I want. My husband doesn't say, 'Look how much money you spend.' I can sit and read a book, work on needlepoint or cook something special, but that really doesn't interest me . . . cooking. It's piddle work. I'm piddling my life away. I got a work kit, Hook Yourself a Rug This Summer, but it's going to be hot lugging that thing around. I have to have something to pass my time. I don't read novels; that requires too much time at one sitting. I read *Time* magazine and the newspaper. I tried short stories—they don't take up too much time—but what happens if I read a novel, I will start it in the evening when it's quiet and read until three in the morning; then I'm exhausted for the next day. So my time is really the worst factor. I want to be selfish about it but how can I be selfish about it when here are all these nice people demanding my time?"

Now, the most well-dressed among us is ready to talk. She's always neatly pressed, as are her identical twin girls.

"I know women who don't have this problem. They're very taken up with their houses, how they look, and that's everything to them. Those women are really quite happy. Or they seem to be." We all suspect she's talking about herself.

"I know a woman who's gone as far as you can go with her house," says the braless mother. "She has motorized the bed, the bar and the drapes. There's a Picasso print over the bidet. Klieg lights outside. They have one of those lackeys outside, too. You know the ones with the lantern, they used to be black men but now they're mostly white. Now she has just intercommed her entire house. She can sit at her breakfast table and with a flip of a switch call to her kids in the bathroom. 'Marie Patrice, did you brush? Herman did you flush?' She doesn't have to set eyes on her kids again except on Christmas morning, when, of course, she'd like to see their surprised and shining little faces."

"I hate mornings, too," says a redheaded woman who has graduated from the playground, except on the days when nursery school is not in session. "When I carpool at nine in the morning, very rarely will I go right home. First of all, I'm suddenly free. There are no more kids with me and I have this freedom, which is going to be taken away at noon. How can you just run out and run back to the house? Some of my neighbors do that and I watch. They're back in seven minutes and I say to myself, how can they do that? It takes so much to get out and then . . . not to even get out of the car. I go to the supermarket or somewhere, do a million errands which are just dumb and then I come home at 10:30 and wonder what to do with myself. Sometimes, out of sheer boredom, I take a nap. There isn't enough time to do anything else in particular so I lie down and go to sleep, so I'll be fresh when the kids come home. I'm already fresh. When they come home and they're playing together, I do very little. It's really just marking time. I watch TV—not soap operas, I made up my mind I would never watch soap operas, so I never did. That has to be the lowest of all the lowly things women do."

The lowly things that women do. It seems, when I listen to us, that we are all badly in need of a destination. To have a life that goes somewhere is a minimal expectation. We need an itinerary instead of just waking up every day (this is the cruelest part) and starting over, as if, hooked up to us is a mental dialysis machine that daily serves up the same old entrée cleansed of memory or sustained purpose. There is nothing carried over from yesterday. No work in progress. No proper life thrust. Without much probing, you can see how attached we are to a few simple heroes of the feminine neuroses—a preoccupation with weight, a sense of disintegration, and a guilt-producing mechanism that, like an automatic ice maker, keeps us filled to capacity.

Are we all here not doing well and finding it out week by week? Will some of us drop like tin soldiers, the others rushing in quickly to close ranks. It's embarrassing. Life erodes our innocence bit by bit. Little tiny time capsules erupt, ready or not, when we can barely stand it. I've certainly run the gamut and each time I thought the information would kill me but it didn't. All the way from finding out that the very nuns who were married to Jesus and wore his simple gold wedding band also wore slightly gray, stretched-out brassieres (with the tacit implication that, as my friend Joanne Press wearily put it, "Nuns have tits just like everybody else") to finding out that lust has very little to do with love and is by far the cleaner of the two emotions.

And who are the pawns in this mindless game? All these little, plump Dorries and Jennies and Susies and Pamelas. These sober-faced Adams and Tommys and Jeffreys and

Brians. All playing innocently while their mothers part the chocolate pudding like Moses parting the Red Sea. We want to cross to the other side. I think.

There is another side to us. There is a point beyond which we will not discuss our problem. We will not open up any can of worms and, I think, for a very good reason. We mistrust our own psyches and have come to believe our own publicity. If we're depressed, we're premenstrual. If we're itchy for a new outlet, we need a good lay. Espouse a cause passionately or semi-passionately and we're ball-breakers. Question any-one—the gas jockey, the pediatrician's nurse, the butcher—the least person—and we're pushy. Pushy is as pushy does. So our lips are sealed. We're admitting nothing.

It was our determination to marry, to bear young that got us here in the first place. We are the prime movers, collec-tively the allied moving and storage company. We have set three, four, five lives in motion, and now to admit the whole system was wrong, the premise wrong, the modus operandi wrong—unthinkable! No. It's much better to talk about other things. White-sale coups, the Bill Blass sheets, the size of our fibroids (all benign when last checked).

There's something else. I think we mistrust each other and our motives. We fear each other, competitors that we are for itchless, odorless, stainless lives. We are afraid that someone, one of us, like Judas Iscariot, will spill the beans. We are not logical beings that can carry an association out logically, the way men do. Like children, we can't be anticipated. We might pounce senselessly on each other, be bitchy, point out cruelly a bad, unfixable trait in one of our children.

I have a recurring dream in which some macho freak on the street sidles up to me and, instead of whispering the usual "MMMMmmm, juicy brown nipples" or "Wanna fuck?" he says, "Hey, Miss. Did you know the life you are leading isn't your own?" I become enraged and want to call a cop. I fear one of these blowsy dames, like the pervert in my dream, will say, "Hey, Sis. Did you know the life you are leading is shit?

You browbeat your kids, your hair is a mess and needs washing, your legs could use a shave and you could lose a few pounds."

But perhaps I am the only one guilty of such thoughts. It's the stinginess oozing out of me. I can't give of myself freely, as the clergy is so fond of advising.

There is a secret stinginess in me and I don't like it. I don't enjoy feeding strangers, and so on. It's not the stinginess I'm aware of that I mind, but I suspect I'm stingy in blind ways that deeply affect my life. Maybe I'm a stingy lover or a stingy cook. What I consider plenty may not be enough. There might be a stinginess in me that is so open and blatant I don't suspect it. There are so many silent decisions. I quiver to think that if my whole system of logic is just a hairsbreadth out of synch, I would be imposing insanity on those around me.

But then it comes to me in a rush of surprise that, of course, I have the mystic and these irritations are simply a special arrangement of energy and, if I will only take the trouble to rearrange the energy, I could eliminate many of them—but stand the chance of eliminating my present life altogether, and that takes some getting used to. Our thoughts are things, the mystic says. Change your thoughts and you will change your experience. Create your future out of the generous dreams of fancy. Imagine better than the best you know.

My mystic, he's not spindly and gaunt like the gurus. He is robust with good color. He faces us simply, wearing a business suit, a proper shirt and tie, sitting on a straight-back chair. His face is an All-American face except for the eyes, strange slanted eyes that see through us, see through life, really, and possibly beyond. We crowd around him, a small intense huddle in the cavernous Laurelton Room, a ballroom on weekends, that seems to echo with shuffling feet, dancing the night away.

At one of the meetings, after a short introductory meditation, a very heavyset man in the audience, with thick, wavy hair that curved around his face like the Cowardly Lion's mane, stood up and faced me. "The walls of your house," he said evenly, "are filled with anger and resentment. The air is thick with fear and anxiety. The next time it rains and each time thereafter, see the rain washing the evil out of your house. Get your children to help you. Tell them to scrub away all unhappiness and imagine the rain making their house clean and free. Also, you don't drink enough water. You're half dead." He sat down abruptly and ignored me for the rest of the lecture.

It has never occurred to me to doubt any of it, just as it has never occurred to me to disbelieve the mystic. Something inside me responds to his truth so readily, it must be he's reminding me of something I already know. But, as it happens, I'm not ready to part with my familiar evils and follow him.

I'm thinking now that Ms. Braless has hit on something. Perhaps what I've been so concerned with is not the issue at all. I'm wondering now, in earnest, what is keeping the family going. What keeps us all conceiving, giving birth, nursing, squawking, bitching, when really so few of us can stand it? Are we feeling the discomfort of desires and instincts that, once dominant, are now recessive? Half in and half out? Perhaps, unbeknownst to me, my number has come up. Today might be that split second in eternity when the mothering juices are no longer running, when the tide has turned. In the days and months and years to come I will cease to care about my young. I will ignore my nest. The bedspreads will be left in a heap. The cake batter will grow a mold. And I, like a wise mother cat, will walk blithely away, viciously dragging one or two kittens that are still clinging to my teats. When Nicholas approaches after ten hours of innocent sleep and stares unblinkingly with eyes so clear the whites are tinged blue and says, "You know what I do with my eyes when I wake up? I do this," and blinks his eyes open slowly, I will turn away without interest. No emotion, mind you. The intent is not to hurt him.

My shoulder will turn cold and I will ignore warm, grubby hands trying to worm their way into mine, full open lips dripping with saliva, a surprisingly throaty voice asking, "Do you want to hear how I sing Oom-pa-pah? First you take the oom and then you take the pah."

"No."

Am I to be the sacrificial lamb on the threshold of a new regrouping; the exact middle-of-the-road point falling on my unsuspecting shoulders? If this is so, then my meanness and resentment are part of the cosmic picture. A necessary evil.

Each time I have a baby I tend to review my life the way one does when drowning, and the tendency is to ask questions: What am I doing here? How did I get to this very important point when I can't remember any momentous preparation?

I gave birth to Andrew on a brisk March night—my least favorite month. With Amanda it was quite different, a dewy July morning and Sunday to boot. But it's not the things I readily like that make me grow. It's the things that cause me pain and trouble. Life is full of conundrums. The rich don't pay taxes. Good junk food is fattening and has no nutritional value. Love is not enough.

I didn't come right out of Nick's birth. I stayed asleep for two days because it took him so long to be born and I tried too hard. D. says the nurse kept slapping my face as I lay there in the corridor, checking my tag to read my name and shouting, "Consuelo, Consuelo. Wake up! You've had a boy."

Even though we followed all the natural business point by point, it's hard to get everyone to keep his word when the moment comes. The doctor is usually tired and cranky and not in the mood to be reminded of hasty promises. They tell you they'll do anything for you, but when you're finally in labor and ask to take the contractions on your knees, someone yanks you down insisting you'll get cramps in your legs or fall out of bed, or both. Nobody takes into account your tremendous ability at that moment. That's one of the chronic circumstances of being a woman. Someone is always telling you they're going to do this or that, but in the end there's a very good reason for not doing it and we nod on the outside but don't much like it on the inside.

With Andrew, my water broke in an art gallery at closing time. "Don't worry," said D. "Nobody notices these things in New York. Just walk along."

It never occurred to me to protest. He put his arm under mine and propelled me along. He persuaded me that we had many hours to wait, so we went to the movies with a stop at Bloomingdale's for towels to contain my oozing uterus.

Thick, thirsty terry, said the ads, and indeed it was. D. didn't care for the colors but I still didn't protest. I waited patiently, running in and out of the ladies' room trying to avoid the attendant's stare even though I was beyond reproach with my belly so far gone. Ironically, the movie we saw was a French film called *The Two of Us*, but I don't remember much of it.

When I look back at their births now, it's with the feeling that something was sprung on me without warning, so I look further back and try to find the seeds and where they were planted and who watered them. To me, it's a strange fruit that grew because totally different seeds were planted. Or so I thought.

I grew up, part of my life, with a velvety-voiced black girl; Corinne Griffith was her name and she came to work for our household when I was thirteen and she was eighteen. She had run away from Little Rock because her Aunt Willie had tried unsuccessfully to have her ovaries removed while telling her it was to be her appendix. "Theah Ah wuz in de docteh's office," said Corinne, "an he's gittin' reddy tuh send me on tuh de hospital. So Ah sez tuh him, 'How come yew knowed muh 'pendix's bad when Ah ain't fult nuthin'?' 'Gurl, Ah ain't tekkin' out yuh 'pendix. It's yuh ovuhries. Ah'm gunna fix it so yew don't get knocked up by uhvery buck in Li'l Rock.' I jes' flew outta dat office. Come straight heah tuh Washington. To Fanny and Flento, de ohny peoples Ah knowed outside Li'l Rock."

Corinne was not cowed by the world, antic though it was for her, and if you came on too strong, she'd say: "Ah ain't studdin' youh Daddy. Ah ain't studdin' youh Mama. An most of all, Ah ain't studdin' yew. So git on outta heah and let me do muh work." All the while she'd be popping marble-sized nuggets of starch into her mouth. She was crazy about clothes starch, the kind that came dry in a box before the whizzy spray-ons.

If you had an argument with Corinne and came around later all hang dog and apologies, she'd say: "Awh shit, yew're awright. Heah's a dollah. Git on down tuh de stohe and git us a big bottle of grape soda and some Dipsy Doodles. They ain't a thin' in this house fit tuh eat. Ah'm gittin' pooher'n Billy Eckstine."

On Billy Eckstine: "He's a singin' fool but yew pick up his trouseh ligs and all yew see is them skinny li'l bird ligs pokin' out." I never asked when exactly she had picked up Billy Eckstine's trouser legs.

On her boyfriend, Tootsie: "Ah ain't studdin' Tootsie. He'll be drivin' dat ole cheekin truck and deliverin' them frozin cheekins when yew and me's moved on to New Yawk and havin' ouwselves a time."

If someone hurt your feelings and you came home all teary: "Don't yew be simple. Don't yew be waitin' on those whiney gurls. Yew'n me's going tuh New Yawk, gurl."

Sometimes on her day off I'd meet Corinne after school in the black ghetto and we'd go visit Fanny and Flento and Baby Flento. Tootsie would come later and pick her up for a date, but he'd always drive me home first in the chicken truck.

There were days when we'd all just be sitting around and visiting together and Tootsie would grab my arm and say, "Mmmmm. This broad's got the softest skin I ever fult. She's gonna make some fool man crazy when she's growed up." I'd go home dreaming my thumping thirteen-year-old dreams. Glad to be a broad. Glad I was going to drive some fool man crazy before too long. Glad to be rid, for the moment, of my own bizarre and complicated dreams and hooked up to ordinary ones. I was glad, too, that it was the end of Corinne's day off and that she'd soon be tugging at my blankets in the morning and yelling at me to "git on outta dat bed."

But deep down, I didn't believe the stuff about driving some fool man crazy nor did I place my hopes on it. One of my fantasies, as if I knew how the world would unfold, was to have my children alone. It wasn't that I had anything against men, I just never bothered to fill in the father face. I worked, of course, and came home to plump, rosy-cheeked toddlers and I was always nice to them. There was nothing in my visions about picking up socks and underwear, taking clothes to the cleaners, scrubbing up endless scum from endless sinks. Like Corinne, I didn't want to be studying anybody and I didn't want to be waiting on any whiney bodies. I wanted the Big Apple and everything that went with it. But my ordinariness came bursting through anyway, like Superman on a mission. I ended up with the whole banana and Corinne stayed on in Washington gobbling starch and downing grape soda with her kids, half legitimate and half illegitimate, crowding in around her.

Chapter Six

TWELVE NOON BY THE TOWN WHISTLE, unmistakable, prodding, but in the end, forgiving.

One of the mental exercises that I do daily involves seeing myself going through the motions of my life as it is now and subsequently seeing the motions as I would like them to be. I would like now to imagine that a friendly, all-knowing reporter is watching us as we leave the playground and reporting what she sees.

The mother and two children piled into the car, a medium-sized foreign car neither old nor new, with a back that opened to provide deck space. The mother threw in their toys—pails, shovels and a very large play bulldozer. She had asked the boy to carry the bulldozer and he had answered that it wasn't a bulldozer but a loader, but he couldn't carry it anyway because he was too tired. She loaded the children into the car and ran back one last time to collect their socks, which they had filled with sand, and beat them against a bench more thoroughly than was necessary. The children did not wait but streamed out again, crying after her. She collected them once more with many reminders that she had to fetch their socks and was coming right back and they knew that and why all the crying? She also muttered half to herself that she must be going crazy to let them go barefoot in April. They continue to whine and cry and she tries to soothe them. "I know you're tired. I know you're hungry."

"I know you tired. I know you tired," mimics the little girl. Her cheeks are round with pleasure at her own sound. She is a pretty child, all one lovely tawny color, with a well-formed body and thick, sturdy legs. The boy, not much larger, has extraordinary eyes, the size and shape as well as the color, which is almost black, iris and pupil as well.

The boy is declining all efforts to be placed in the car and finally agrees to be picked up as a passenger at a "bus stop" several yards away.

"You be the bus and I'll be the rider," he says. "Then when you get close to me, say 'all the boreds' and then say 'tickets, please. May I have your tickets, please?' Then I'll give you my ticket and you give the change, OK?"

"OK. But it's 'all aboard,' not 'all the boreds.' " She smiles to herself. Huh. All the boreds. None of you excited guys . . . out of the mouths of babes.

The woman is not well-groomed, but now, standing beside the car trying to make quick decisions about how to work it with the youngsters, she looks fatigued as well. There are snatches of chic: wide-legged pants, large sunglasses, an expensive ski jacket. She is carrying a large, tri-colored canvas handbag, obviously a leftover from other summers, with the word "Vote" printed on it, although there is no election in progress. "It's a perfectly good bag," she explains to her husband each time he protests that it doesn't make sense to keep on carrying it. Just the same reasoning she had used when she came home with a fistful of greatly reduced brassieres from Bloomingdale's, each with a raunchy saying on the left cup. Silly things like, "Just the Two of Us." "We Make a Great Pear."

The canvas bag is a little soiled, as are her shoes, as is her car, as are the children, although you can't say they're neglected. The large dark glasses give her a certain mystery and also, I suppose, allow her some privacy with her emotions.

She drives up to where the boy is standing and says, "Tickets, please."

"Mo-o-m." His cheeks get puffy and his eyes fill with tears. He has no patience now for dialogue misplaced. "You didn't say 'all the boreds' first."

"OK. Close the door and we'll try it again." She is obviously pleased with her continued good humor. They try it again and this time it goes well. The boy gets in.

They drive home in silence, the girl sucking her thumb, making a staccato but not unpleasant grunt between sucks. When they are within a few blocks of home, the boy says, "Go Winding Way" and the girl says, "Go straight." She goes straight and the boy begins to rail and punch her lightly on the shoulder with his small fist.

"You never do anything," he says. He means, of course, that she never does anything for him, but he simply says, "You never do anything."

"That isn't true, Nicky," she answers, but inside she considers that perhaps he is right. Perhaps she never does do anything. This comes with today's suspicion (becoming increasingly strong as the day wears on) that she is not judging her performance with the solid scale of sanity. Not playing with a full deck, as they say. D., her husband, has the same complaint. They're not doing enough. He feels at loose ends. They should see more people. Go to more movies. Perhaps, she thinks, there is an impotence that's quite obvious to everyone and she's just going along uncaringly confident that everything is right.

A police car with the siren on comes along and distracts them all. The boy from his disgruntlement and the mother from her thoughts. She pulls aside to let it pass.

"Is he going for a robber?" asks the boy.

"Yes," says the mother.

"Can we see him?" asks the boy.

"No," says the mother.

"Maybe it's an emergency," says the boy.

"Yes. Could be," says the mother.

"Could we see it?"

"No. It wouldn't be something you'd want to see. It would be terrible. And maybe someone hurt and cars smashed. It's no fun to see an accident."

"You never do anything." Although you're not supposed to react to children, supposed to stay above it all, she feels the message hammered home.

They are following a truck and she allows her imagination to be engaged by the message on the back: "Delivering another fine printing job by George Dunlop," says the truck. The self-serving signs have been sprouting up lately. "Another fine renovation by Michael Christie." "Another dream-come-true pool by Sheldon In-Ground Pools." Everything is geared to keep morales high, ambitions on edge. Keep the dream ever before you and you'll survive the rough spots. But what was the dream? Did anybody remember?

It was a tired and hungry bunch that rolled in after a busy morning.

That is indeed a friendly and accurate report that I myself would have colored with unnecessary adjectives and dire predictions, which only goes to show that D. is right. It's not what happens that's important but how you take it. However, the last sentence has made me grab back the reins. Nobody talks that way anymore. We know now that fatigue is mainly emotional and hunger is multileveled. Only a Lipton Soup commercial would talk that way. We are actually, now, jockeying for position, manning our battle stations. They want me. I want me, too. Alone. To myself. I don't want to do anything to them or for them any longer and I don't want to be mature about it. On the other hand, I don't want them to know I don't want them. I want them to think that I want only them. And I worry that the tone of my voice is too cloying, joining in their singsong pettiness. Does Nicky want his eggy-egg? Nicky's going to have a nice lunch and take a resty-rest.

We're all stuck together living in a fisheye lens of a world, twisting and winding about each other, a take-off on Bosch or Brueghel. Our features are so close we look distorted, eyes browner than life, more liquid than life. We spend our time singing our silly songs. To market to market to buy a fat pig. Home again, home again, jiggety jig. Something makes me say that each time we turn into our driveway. We push swings and count. Seesaw. Margery Daw. They love the repetition. They thrive and squeal on the known. The safe. They turn in anger and bewilderment if you change one word, move one comma. It's not funny. They can't take a joke.

There are many ways to do it. There is time alone waiting for me just on the other side of the hill. Time to read a book, to gobble down a solid sandwich, to worship over a double-decker cone without saucer eyes and dripping lips limning my every lick. Time to curl up in the big Eames chair deliciously alone and . . . what? Read a magazine, make short work of the vacuuming, make long work of straightening out drawers.

Do they know I mean to dump them in their beds and hope they sleep on and on? Not to refresh them, certainly, but simply to free me. I want to be free of them. It's strange that when I was single and had no one to love, thoughts of love dominated everything. Now that I'm a wife and mother with many love dependencies, love, like size 33 hips, is no longer an issue.

There is time alone waiting for me just on the other side of the hill and I'm coming over the hill like John Wayne or Van Johnson. Crawling my way to the crest on my belly to throw the decisive grenade. I feel the small things in the ground digging reassuringly into my cotton fatigues. There are many ways to do it. I can feed them food they won't balk at—sections of orange, bits of cheese, a frosty treat made in the blender with frozen berries, an egg snuck in. I can seduce them into their beds with Playtex bottles, the closest thing structurally to mother's breast. I can trick them into sleep with the sound of their favorite book . . . "Sam Cat and Dudley Pig were very fine detectives . . ." Then I will be alone, perfectly still to plan my life. Before me is a stunning mirage. I hear the sirens calling each to each. The mermaids purposely hum a haunting song. "Why the swim upstream, my dear? Come with us."

As if to punctuate my thoughts, the phone rings. It is D. calling. He doesn't want me to swim upstream either. He wants me to go with the tide. He wants to know if I have called the Riddleys or, a sudden new entry, the Stills. If I'm doing anything to repair the hole in our life.

"I just want to know how you're doing." D. calls daily to see how I'm doing, but today there's an edge to his voice. Hesitation. I know that voice. The nuances. Each twist and turn of intention. Does he want to veil his intentions from me the way I want to veil my intentions from the children? Does he want to be free?

But what to tell him? What do I need with the Riddleys if I decide to stop? To wind the clock no longer? If I decide to picture myself alone again in a completely orderly house, functioning from initiative instead of reacting, forever reacting? What if I decide to resort to my own sweet magic and leave him to his logic and the ways of the world?

I think of his strong competent hands holding the phone. Long nimble fingers innocent of dicing onions and slicing carrots and kneading dough. Clumsy with the children's tiny buttons, their tiny clothes. Unfamiliar with dust mops, stuffing clothes into washers and dryers. The oven a strange country.

"I haven't called anyone."

"Why not? It's already late to call someone for Saturday. Maybe we should make it Friday or Sunday, although Sunday would be my last choice."

It seems such a silly thing for an issue. Call the Riddleys. Don't call the Riddleys. What's the difference?

If this were a novel, one of my children would die or be very sick. Or my husband would die or be very sick. Or he would be in an accident or his business would collapse or he'd start drinking. Or have an affair with his secretary. Or with his boss. There are so few possibilities for outward human tragedy. If there are only four tastes and, as designers say, only four basic dress silhouettes, perhaps there are only four basic human situations and all that extraordinary individualism we're so fond of is merely a variation on a very boring theme. Perhaps if we run from any one of these situations, we're doomed to repeat it until we work it out.

If this were a novel, perhaps I, the heroine, would be very sick or die. Or I might be relegated to a distracting subplot. Comic relief. The more important theme being the aloneness itself. The splendid solitary condition of man/woman and how all their lives they seek escape into companionship, togetherness, sensation, security. How all their lives (ha, ha) they try to live it up.

In a novel I would be dealt with metaphorically. I would be dumped like excess fuel or jettisoned like a targetless bomb in mid-ocean or on a deserted isle or in a deserted relationship or in a brave new world where the rules were all strange and every time I learned a rule it would no longer be operative. However, as it happens in reality, I have no ready denouement. I have to artificially accelerate my craziness, my bitchiness, my insanity, in order to create a chilling climax. A turning point.

I know what D. would say if he knew what I was up to. He would say, "You want issues? I'll give you issues." But he doesn't know. His voice is uncluttered by anxiety. He obviously does not yet know that he is at my mercy.

"Will you *do* something? I don't want to spend this Saturday watching Mary Tyler Moore. Our lives are becoming a closed, tight circle. Don't make it an elaborate thing. One dish

. . . lasagna or something, crusty French bread, a nice salad." My God, I think, he's turned into Nancy Nice, home economist.

"I am not going to do anything," I reply, taking a certain joy in being unreasonable. How cold and contained can my voice be. "I'm not going to call anyone or have anyone to dinner or do absolutely anything except feed and shelter these children until I decide once and for all what it is I am really . . . or rather ultimately going to do. Possibly I'll feed you, too, if you stop telling me to *do something*, which does not mean, as it should, to take the whole realm of possibility and do something that will be good for me but just something that will distract me."

Then, as he always does, D. creates a little trap for me. "Do you think you'd be happier living alone in some apartment in New York? What would you do with the children? Where would they play? You think they're driving you crazy now, how do you think they would do cooped up in a three-room apartment with nowhere to go? No outside. Or . . ." He pauses before the kill: "Weren't you planning to take the children?" He gives as much of a sneer as he is capable of giving, which is not much. "You can't even leave them for an evening without worrying all night whether they were reminded to pee, if they got their drink, their story, their night light."

"Do you think I baby them too much?"

"Yes. Yes, I do." Through the irritation and growing sense that my argument has turned against me, my heart gives a thump of gladness that he thinks I display this much tenderness to the children. I'm still addicted to ratings. I want a reading on how I'm doing even while I'm mooning about the day I'll finally pull the rug out from under it all.

This tactic of D.'s is known as the old one-two. First ask her an unanswerable question. Then give her the answer. I'm stunned because I don't know how to continue. I have nothing better to say.

There are many things wrong with this marriage but none of them conclusive. Then, too, D. is ready and willing to try and believes we have a solid foundation. There is nothing dreadful going on. I'm quite alone in my suspicion that a denouement is needed here. "I can call the sitter if you like and we can go out to dinner. We can take the Riddleys out to dinner." D. is speaking in a soft conciliatory voice.

"No, no. Let me think about it. That's not the whole thing . . . calling the baby sitter."

So let's see what we've got here. I'm making the Riddleys and the stuffing down of some pork chops *à la chinoise* and the downing of an undistinguished St. Emilion and talk about how crummy the kid's teacher is and what are our plans for Earth Day or Food Day or whatever the hell has turned up to engage their enthusiasm—I'm making that the pivotal issue on which to hang my life plan. Not only my life but theirs, his, and all the peripheral people whose little routines would run willy-nilly like Uncle Wiggley's round of cheese down Christmas Tree Hill.

But what else to make the pivotal issue? The birdseed? Or the lack of birdseed? And if not the Riddleys, how else to fill my days? My mornings? My afternoons? Writing riddles for television commercials? Riddles or the Riddleys. The Lady or the Tiger. To say nothing of THE CHILDREN. They cannot be disposed of as easily as the Riddleys. I will remember how they look before they cry. Before they laugh. Before they nibble at their bread in such an endearing way. The little crunches of tiny sharp teeth taking tiny sharp bites.

Whom am I railing against like little Nick? Whom am I punching with small ineffectual fists? If I would explain all this to D., he would simply take me in his arms and say, "Oh, poor dear. I didn't realize it was like this. What can we do together to make it better?"

We can't do anything together to make it better because it's my problem. A boring identity problem.

It's true what he says about leaving the children. The more

I am with them, the less I want to leave them with baby sitters. When I think about all of the times I've been away from them, it feels like a lapse of memory and it occurs to me with relief that I was lucky to come back and find them alive and in one piece. The feeling is that I had this little baby and I forgot about it for a week but then remembered it with such fright and wondered if it was still alive. When it turned out nothing had happened, such a relief and a promise never to let it out of my sight again.

Now I have been very careful about listening to mothers when they talk about leaving their children, and there is a running thread of terror.

One woman said: "When Robbie was born, when he was very little, before I had the other children and I left him with someone, I would come running back. Sometimes I'd run for three or four blocks . . . I was sure something had happened to him or that he needed me very badly. I ask him now—he's eight—was there ever a time when you wanted your mother very badly? When you just really wished with all your heart that she was there? He said just one time, 'the first day I stayed in school all day and had my lunch. You put a note in the lunchbox and it said you were thinking about me and loved me. I couldn't stand it. I wanted you to be there so badly, right next to me. There was nothing I could do about it.' I got the idea about the note from one of those books. 'Put a little note in his lunchbox,' it said; 'It will comfort him.' It just shows you those books don't tell you anything."

Meg Riddley (whom D. would like to see dining with us this weekend) puts it this way: "I don't think of anyone else except myself as being a really good person who can take care of them. My husband . . . maybe 85%, he's 85% as good as me but he doesn't have their routine down as pat. The thing is they've had very good times with sitters and certainly with their father but . . . I leave long lists and five thousand numbers where we can be reached. They've always been fine. There's no saying that if I'm not there everything has to be exactly the same, but in my innards, I think that if I'm not there, particularly if I'm not there, it must absolutely be as it is when I am there. Otherwise it will be—" a long pause "—I don't know, wrong . . . menacing."

Ann Sheridan's look-alike puts it this way: "Some of the things that frustrate me, one of the big things, is my time. Say, if there is an activity that I enjoy doing, it is maybe for two hours somewhere. I can never find the time. It is so difficult to plan a day. Going into the city for the day is a good example. I have to make arrangements for the children, and, if I do, I know it is going to end at such and such a time and it makes me feel guilty because it makes me feel selfish. There is always guilt involved. Whatever you do that you enjoy you feel guilty. If I go away with my husband on a vacation, there's guilt because I'm leaving the children at home and maybe it will ruin them forever. Who knows what damage it will do? Then there's always that time schedule. My time involves everybody's time and yet, my husband, and again I feel guilty because it isn't his fault—he's got that freedom."

The psychologists say when you have pervasive fears about the safety of your children it usually means you'd like to do harm to them yourself.

D.'s last words ring in my ears. "Do it for me. Call the Riddleys for me. OK?" And when there's no answer from me, click. Gone.

He would never force me to do anything and yet his fairness is itself an arm twister. He wouldn't even hold a grudge if I didn't do anything. He wouldn't sulk or be hostile all weekend. He might sigh a couple of times toward evening and say, "What's it all about?" but he wouldn't call me a bitch and tell me to get on the fucking phone and call somebody instead of sitting here feeling so sorry for myself. He would never say that. It isn't his way.

The thing is, I don't feel sorry for myself. I really don't. I feel sorry for them and I do have a plan of action or at least a hope of a plan of action, but it's going to take a little time and how can I expect him to wait and be patient when I can't promise that the outcome will be in his favor? Of course, it will be in his favor in the ultimate sense, whatever I do. If I jump on the band wagon and put my all into this life of ours it will be in his favor in the immediate sense. If I decide to fade off, either physically or mentally, it will be in his favor in the ultimate sense because, although the next few weeks may be unbearable, at least he'll be working from a solid platform and not with such shaky equipment as myself to hang his hopes on.

Such a puny revolt. Just whether or not on this particular day you will continue to play the game, plan for company dinner, bathe your children, kiss your husband when he comes home from the office. What a silly issue. But maybe not so silly.

Of course, D. is right. Where would I go with my children? He has even brought up the possibility that I might not take the children. Does that mean he would fight for them? I know right now, as if I were already ensconced in my dingy $3\frac{1}{2}$ rms, that I would be happy to see him when he came. But what can I expect from him? Will he turn callous and grim? I am not absolutely certain who he is. If I've been looking at him myopically, I've only seen what is acceptable. He's just a stranger capable of all the things strangers are capable of. He can nudge me out of the way, grabbing the last of the merchandise out of my hands because he doesn't have to meet my gaze at dinner. Vacantly killing me off like an unseen enemy because he has never met my mother or watched me with my children. The thought comes to me often that I'm confronting a stranger whose sense of ethics is only operative where he is known and has a continuing relationship. And I don't know him. He's not a blood relative (no wonder we want to marry Daddy). He's somebody I picked up ten years ago, and I've been so busy, busy as a bee, learning to cope with lessening emotions, with mounting emotions. Learning to practice emotional acupuncture. How to mimic happiness, joy, expectation, hope, humaneness. But now that I'm beginning to believe in my reality, I'm worried about my safety. I'll just have to sniff him out. Wait and see.

My friend is outside. I'm looking out at Libby in her battered Chevy Nova, a depressing gold, and I see a new, ugly dent on the right front fender. She is carrying a sleeping Joshua in her arms.

"He fell asleep on the way," she says sheepishly as I open the door. "Can I put him down somewhere? He's not going to like waking up in a strange house but maybe he'll stay asleep until I get back." I lead the way to Amanda's bedroom, where there is an extra bed, and she arranges the sleeping Joshua.

It's impossible not to notice how impeccable Libby is in her tennis whites and it occurs to me that she is a fastidious person with herself and with her house. It's not something you think about right away with Libby because she's so relaxed and open about herself. I remember how many times she has commented on what she calls our "carefree" ways. Piles of newspapers strewn about, the children mostly always barefoot, sometimes without coats in the dead of winter. She says it's a good, healthy attitude on my part and deplores her own neatness as a compulsion. But now I'm feeling a bit ashamed of how I look, and to further complicate my feelings we pass the laundry room and she takes in the mountains of laundry piled near the door.

"If you only had someone in to do the fucking laundry and fold it and put it in the fucking drawers," she says vehemently. "You'd be surprised what that would do for you."

"Yeah." I am beyond her suggestions. "But that's not the answer. You've always had good help. Your mother must have had good help."

"She did," she looks at me mildly surprised. "You're right, she always did."

"We never had good help. Either very fancy and neurotic or I made them my mother substitute and wanted to do their work. That's what I do now. I confide in them and give them all my clothes. After a few weeks, they stop working altogether."

"That ends that."

"How is it with you?"

"Depends on when you ask. Right now, fine. When I'm off like this to play tennis and then maybe for a civilized low-calorie lunch, it's great. When I have to return to my four gorgeous walls—Antique Satin according to the Dutch Boy catalogue, reminiscent of wedding bells and encrusted with tradition—then the little gremlins inside me start stirring things up." She puts her hands on her hips, further hiking up her ridiculously short tennis dress. "Why don't I like staying home with my children?" Just asking the question brings her solace and she doesn't really want an answer.

"There's a big dent on your car. What happened?"

"Oh, that. I guess I wanted to punish Barry for something. He mowed over all my asparagus plants last week and I smashed up the car to get even. Just a nice neat dent, nothing serious. Nobody hurt."

"You think it's tit for tat, huh?"

"He resents my gardening, I resent his being away from the house so much, and there you are, a nice setup for a psychodrama."

"But where does free will, our will, come in?"

"Who says we have any . . . well, maybe some, but certain things are obvious whether you choose to look at them in that way or not."

"And you think it's all right to live that way, two little subconscious freaks battling it out below decks?" I have an immediate image of Libby's impish creature and Barry's sober-faced one dueling it out while Libby and Barry carry on their mannered life—a long-running Sheridan play.

"If you're onto a better way, I'm certainly open to suggestions." She turns and heads for the door, eager to be on her way. Having dropped her sleeping burden, she's suddenly young and carefree.

What if I *am* onto a better way? What if I were to tell Libby that I have a marvelous new way to straighten out my life and arrange my future to my own satisfaction? That each day can be filled with joy? And suppose good old, practical Libby asked me, "OK, let's start with a rainy day and the kids all home from school. How would you handle a rainy day when they're glassy-eyed from the television and feeling bitter and bored?" She would look me straight in the eye, full of confidence.

"I would go through the day, imagining exactly how I wanted it to go. I would live in the feeling of the wish fulfilled and all the ideas I would need to cope with it would come to mind." It doesn't sound right explained like that. Then, too, my life, at the moment, is not a good example of how effective the mystic's teachings really are.

What's behind all this crummy behavior, this need to showcase my struggles, my sacrifices? Is it that I want to punish him for giving me what I wanted in the first place? Tit for tat, as Libby contends? Punish him for where we live. What we eat. When we go to bed. Where we go on vacation. What paper we read. What movies we see. When the lights go out. Do I want to punish him because I say I'm sorry when the children are too loud or when the laundry breaks the buttons on his shirts? Who gets the bathroom first? Whose needs come first? I'm not as sure as he is as to what I want, so I demur and defer. Quite unbidden and unnoticed, I gave over the reins of my life. Nobody asked for them, we just . . . well . . . we fell into a pattern, as they say. I can't impose my will on him because my wants and needs and preferences are distorted now from lack of use. At this stage I might cut off my nose to spite my face. Impose something irrational just to have my say and, of course, it would become an issue. The next time it would be an issue as well. And the third and fourth times, too. I can't live through four issues. So, instead, I pick some small thing to detonate me—his being late for dinner or slow to anger, or slow to answer.

He is a shadowy figure in our lives. Living, paradoxically, for the work that provides him a living. Parading at home as the handyman, the elusive provider, the hard-to-pin-down prime mover of our lives. I can't blame him for that. We're both merely casualties of race momentum. Innocent victims of the same faceless assailant.

I've lost my wedding ring three times. The first was on the ski slopes (a sport I took up at his urging) at the bottom of a loathsomely difficult trail, a trail so narrow that four of us had toppled, domino fashion, when a man at the top came sliding down on his back, safety bindings holding like Elmer's Glue-All. At the bottom, I took off my mitten, shook my hand and watched my simple gold wedding band make a graceful arc in the air before burying itself forever in a four-month accumulation of soft powdery snow. We scratched around for a while with our ski poles, but my heart wasn't in it. Perhaps, in the spring, a vacationing single would find it and see it as an omen.

The second time I lost my ring (a less innocent model this time with mythological markings on red enamel) it fell into a pile of leaves I was raking on our property—his dream property, which I find lonely to a fault but had agreed to enthusiastically (the way I agree to everything) in a daze of acquiescence and robot good will, which prevails until I get my period, at which time I see everything more clearly than I wish to. They say we get bitchy at menstrual time but I believe our bodies emit a truth serum that allows us clear vision once a month and we become furious at what we see.

The third and last time (I don't wear a ring anymore) I don't remember losing the ring. One day, I looked down and it was gone. No need to delve for symbolism here.

Chapter Seven

IT MUST BE 2:10, at most 2:15, because I hear the mailman's jeep stopping and starting on the road. There is no clock here. I am lying on the thickly carpeted floor of my laundry/sewing/project center, legs stretched flat out, back leaning against a dryer still warm from the last load.

The children are asleep and I am hallucinating. I'm chasing the blues away, chasing the blues away. I'm creating gospel like Matthew, Mark, Luke or John. Good news. Just recently I learned that gospel means good news.

For two months, I have been looking inside myself and I am so delighted I can barely cope with the excitement. I still my mind and body to the degree that all thought and energy converge to one central focus. Then I wait and look. Not in a formal way—I'm too timid for TM. At first, I see myself sitting in a cell-like room hugging my knees, not an unpleasant room, monastic in content with thick stucco walls and a heavy oak door with an unconventional handle that makes a reassuring clunk when it closes. Outside the door, the shoulds of my life lie limp in a heap, like so many two-dimensional derelicts in an early Dali painting.

I live alone in my thoughts. This is thinking as I've never known it. Ephemeral at first but progressively more potent. Full of life. Having direction and power.

After a few minutes I can see the shell of my body, comfortable but detached, as my palpable spirit takes flight and moves off to more rewarding worlds. I watch myself in the third person. Treat my life like a shallow script being cranked out on a Moviola, easy to splice and change. See my life as a series of choices that could be easily replaced by other choices were I to take the trouble. See the hubbub of my daily itinerary as so much static that could be tuned out and replaced by something equally removable. See love choices that outlive the love and can be set aside without emotion, displaced by more current love choices—love of me, for instance. See emotion, as I know it, as a barrier to growth, self-inflicted because I'm too lazy to keep on going beyond the obvious and familiar.

This essence transcends sex and circumstance. It becomes my desires. It becomes strangers who give me succor, faces I wouldn't recognize in my objective world. They give me a hand to wherever I want to go, no questions asked. I climb higher and higher. Just by being still, I can feel a part of me pervading other bodies. Pervading situations and becoming situations. Becoming feeling. It must have been like that when we were just born.

I have been taking refuge more and more these days in this world while my "real" world, my mechanical world, takes on dreamlike qualities and at the same time becomes more real because I can watch it without involvement. I go about my chores with my pulse connected to that which animates me, that center to which the chatty ring is tied. I'm surprised and disconcerted that it's been there all along while I went blindly through my paces for the last umpteen years.

Momentarily it takes the fear out of everything. Whatever I must do to right myself, I can handle. Like crazy Ophelia, pushing her hair out of her eyes, hoisting her nightgown so as not to trip, carrying a dripping candle to light her way, I have begun a journey. It's a precarious business all the way but a different security is bolstering me up.

It's not all child's play, however, The world crowds in—

root canal work, wine stains that won't come out, outgrown shoes and outgrown social scenes. I lose touch.

I'm not putting my attention on the problem of the dinner party. I'm letting the day slip away, the immediacy of it, and that won't do. Today has to be the day or no day will be the day. D. is going to sit in his chair and as we share a lamp and read together I will feel his restlessness. He'll rise two or three times and walk briskly toward the medicine cabinet or to the kitchen sink. Or he'll rub his stomach absently under his waistband, an action that has special significance (body language).

Why is it that one minute the day seems long and endless and in another few minutes the whole irrational illusion of time comes crashing down and you realize it's already too late? Either I will do what I must to keep from driving D. into some slimy social limbo or I will do something to dramatically point out to him that he can no longer depend on my holding up my half. Either tell him to look out for himself, or do something myself.

The other thing is that it hasn't been clearly established who it is we want to know. Whom we should be wining and dining. D. claims we always react to people who want to know us. We're batted around by whoever needs us to round up their parties. Yet I'm sure we must want to know and court someone. There must be people out there we would want very badly to know if we knew of them. Someone to trot out our best behavior for, our charm, our *Caneton au Grand Marnier*.

I just remembered something, oh God. He's despairing over something else. D. looks down the road of life, a life with me, and sees it as . . . what? Empty. Lived out with a balking hulk having to be urged, anticipated, hoodwinked into sex. A pseudo-innocent never returning inviting glances, always wide-eyed when she should be knowing. It isn't the lack of dinner parties; it's life with me.

When I began going to the mystic I had been feeling rather bad, not enough energy, sleeping most evenings away right after supper. We couldn't figure it out; physically I was fine. I even had my teeth checked because I had heard of three different people who were very sick, only hours from death if you could believe the story, and it was their teeth, though nobody thought to look.

Tired of being tired, I was guru-bound, fast becoming a social oddity. The housewife as mystic adjusting her supersheer Supp-Hose to accommodate a meditational position. Who could better bring respectability to these brash promises?

I explored my inside world like a child in an expensive candy store (no penny gumballs for me), heady with the idea that everything begins and ends with me. The only possibilities were those that occurred to me. My view of life went lickety-split down a narrow road, and I shuddered to think what else was available to me.

The mystic said that the moment we die, instantaneously we will see two beings—one horrendous and one beautiful— and the horrendous one will be made up of our instant chagrin when we realize what a minuscule portion we saw and used of life. The beautiful creature would be our good deeds (not the Boy Scout variety), times when we used our imagination even if the world didn't agree. He said in many different ways that our fantastic imagination was the key to the whole thing and to develop our fantasy-making powers because that was the only true gift humans had.

His words coaxed me into a coma of reverie and imaginal calisthenics. It sobered me to think that were I to be born a hundred years hence, I would be many times less limited than I am now. That I am living on the threshold of a new description of life and my constant, unappreciated bitching is not seen for what it is—a clarion call. I am the advance man stirring things up for a new visitation.

When I think of my imaginal activities thus far, I realize the gift has been lost on me. It doesn't take much sentry work to sum up the big themes in my life. The table of contents reads like this: How will it be when I'm serene, completely sure, skinny, relaxed, rich, more socially powerful? How will it be when my mouth is perpetually relaxed? The tension throughout my entire body seems to be controlled by the tight set of my mouth. This is where my suspicion of foul play is physically manifested, leaving the rest of me to do what is expected.

But you will say: Ridiculous. You're raising a family, it will pass. Or the religionists will say: Help others. True satisfaction will come from helping others. Obliterate the self and lose the self in selfless work. The metaphysicians will say: Guard your thoughts. Be as careful what you allow in your mind as what you allow in your stomach. Garbage in. Garbage out. Albert Ellis will say: Eliminate the *should*s in your life. Shouldhood leads to shithood.

The mystic is gone now. I called recently to find out when he would return; the woman who answered said he had crossed over. Made his transition. They don't like to say anyone's dead. They say the person has crossed over. But the woman on the phone—foreign, maybe French—she thought I needed comforting and told me there had been nothing wrong physically. The mystic just burned himself up with light and understanding. So now I'm just left with what he gave me. Some is carefully written down, some is carefully stored in my head. It's hard to believe what the mystic says and there doesn't seem to be an appropriate way of recounting it. No matter how you put it, it sounds absurd to say you can have whatever you want just by thinking about it. A very special kind of thinking. No one will sit still and listen to that, although I took to it right away. When he spoke, it was Velcro parting in my brain (that miracle fabric that locks to itself yet parts again so easily); that's how my mind is when the mystic speaks.

The mystic tells me I've been looking for power and security—*i.e.*, good news—up the wrong alley. I've been hanging my hopes on the world of Nelson Rockefeller's presidential aspirations, Handi-Wipes, Chevy Estate Wagons, *The New York Times*, Scott's Turf Builder and Billy Graham. Not that any of these wouldn't conform to the idea that life is what you make it. But the mystic, he wasn't afraid to go out on a limb. He said I could crank out the details of my future like an intoxicated organ grinder with an independent income. What's more, I could undo any part of my past by simply reconstructing it imaginally in a way that would promote my well-being. The pruning shears of revision, he called it.

I could reconstruct a less compulsive mother, an affectionate father, a great social life in high school. Limited only by consciousness and desire, I could think myself rich, thin, happy, loved, separated, alone, divorced, married, in Europe, in good health, in heaven. It all took place inside. Causation, he said, was neither governmental, nor chemical, nor religious, nor parental, nor inevitable. It was, first and foremost, imaginal.

You could flip back a mental calendar and snuggle up to Daddy to your heart's content and forever after cease searching for him the world over. Conversely, you could put together a new, non-man-eating Mommy and escape the old one's suffocating grasp. You could persuade uncaring parents to become interested as hell. You could explore all the crevices of your parents' bodies and burrow into every one. Finally, you could crawl out and visualize, very simply, taking the reins of your own life (seeing the reigns, if you liked). "On, Dancer, On, Comet, On, Donner and Blitzen." Of course, when you arrived topside, up from your fantasy, all kinds of subtle changes would have taken place and you would be on a different footing than before.

"How many mental trips does a human being make?"

"As many as it takes to convince yourself," answered the mystic.

There is a lot of talk around the mystic about the stillness of the soul. The sound of one hand clapping. The inner ear. It is the chatter of his disciples who cannot cope with the simplicity of his message. They talk about karma and soul molds. The mystic, on the other hand, is very concise and to the point. He tells us how to get things and his reputation rests on that. Where else should you look for what you want but to yourself, he says.

Unfortunately, he is tiring of telling people how to get fur coats, Arthur Murray franchises, new houses, new husbands, money or winning tickets at the races. His heart isn't in it. He wants to lead us to higher ground but we're not ready to go. I, for one, have visions of Gucci and Pucci dancing in my head.

The routine is, of course, to quiet the mind by whatever method—counting backward, repeating a phrase, breathing deeply—until one feels a floating sensation and then, in that state, to picture vividly, in an imaginary scene, the wish fulfilled. To abandon one's self to the feeling of the wish fulfilled. The more sensory and emotional detail poured into the picture, the better. If money is the wish (everyone thinks immediately that money will be everyone's wish, but many times it is not), we have to see stacks of it lying about, big balances in our checkbooks. He was telling us that wishing did make it so, provided it was done in the spirit of "thank you," rather than in the spirit of "please." After all, didn't the Bible say: "What things soever ye desire, when ye pray, believe that ye receive them, and ye shall receive them"? We were to keep mentally inhabiting this waking dream, returning to it several times a day until it became fact in our lives. Keep cashing in the winning tickets at the winner's window. Keep kissing the desired husband "good morning" and "good night." Keep walking around the house of our dreams, touching and feeling the things we loved best.

What he couldn't tell us, because we weren't ready to hear it, was that our inner landscape would be one of the more startling discoveries. That we would fall in love with ourselves and see what great and curious beings we were. That we were as gods, for god's sakes.

The first thing that occurs to me in today's meditation, as it always does, is to lose weight. Now, even while hurting and wondering what is to become of me, my gut response is to lose weight. Shallow, shallow. I'm still scrambling after a life plan orchestrated by Johnny One-Note. At eighteen be popular. At twenty-five be married. At thirty be rich. At thirty-five be thin.

For starters, I want to weigh one hundred pounds soaking wet, like Amanda Burden. To put to rest the notion that only homely women are complicated and searching, that a beautiful woman has simple needs easily met—to be pampered, adored and always fit into what she puts on in the morning. I want to inspect my bone structure. How can I hope to decipher the meaning of happiness when I have never seen my adult bone structure?

My obsession is with thinness. You can never be too thin or too rich said the Duchess of Windsor. Keep yourself emaciated and unapproachable. With me, however, it isn't a true obsession or I wouldn't be expert at keeping myself fat. If I were thin, I could walk into a room and be aware and interested in what was in the room instead of how I look walking into the room.

My first and only analyst, a rerouted rabbi, swore to me that we hid unresolved situations in different parts of our body and in later life these became the lumpy deposits of fat that no amount of exercise or starvation could dissolve. Daddy love was stuck in the thighs. Mother hate in the hips. Death fear in the gut. Life fear in the chest. He didn't actually swear these theories to me, just nodded approvingly in that maddening way of analysts when question by question you unravel their theories and serve them up like a five-course meal while they eat lazily away.

The first step in my self-improvement, life-improvement

schedule is an ultimate confrontation with my face and figure to decide once and for all what is possible and what is not. To confront the firm, farm-healthy fat that has dribbled its way into my body while I ooh'd and aah'd at my newborns —a time when I literally put my mind in cold storage while I psyched up my breasts to produce milk. (Up yours, La Leche!)

I want to dig out my thighs and bottom from every ounce of extra fat and see what is really there. Maybe the Estée Lauder woman is there, cool and unapproachable, with her independent wealth and stingy smile. It isn't so much vanity as an insatiable curiosity over the original potential before the layers of protective fat began to cover me up.

There is a sequence to creation, even creating a new me, and the first step is the tearing down. Peel off the layers of toughened skin that I've grown in self-protection, and the first surprise I come to is a murderous anger. Yes, nice little me. Little mother wants to kill, kill, kill.

When I worked in advertising, there was a popular sticker around of a noble beast, a cultured beast with a beautifully shaped mane and a long, well-bred nose. The caption beneath said simply: Kill. Kill. Kill. Scratch the cookie-maker and you find murder. A provocateur of emotions, now hoisting up, now letting down. I have been angry so long I am not acquainted with any other emotion. If I lose weight and get in touch with all my nerve endings, I'll end up a demented sniper killing off those around me like clay pigeons. Then I'll be a skinny murderess arousing the interest of thousands of men who read the front page of the *Daily News*. I think the maternal urge to kill is at bottom an affirmation of life. The producer of life is the taker of life. If I don't lose weight, I will remain a nice scatterbrained lady who cries sometimes to get attention.

What alerted me to this self-loathing? My eldest had brought home seven little cardboard signs from school that read: "Hi, friend!" His teacher had given them to the class with the suggestion that they be placed against all bathroom mirrors and each child, in passing, should look himself firmly in the eye and say, "Hi, friend."

We all wanted to try it but, in my case, the words stuck in my throat. When I tried to coax myself into a benign, friendly mood, rage came out. I have been nice all my life, except to my mother, and now I couldn't even say, "Hi, friend" to my mirror image. I could say, "Hi, martyr. Hi, brain. Hi, fatso. Hi, wit. Hi, schmuck."

I am definitely not my friend, but it helps to know I'm an honest enemy and certainly not hypocritical. Why this self-loathing? What is it that I don't particularly like? How can I like my husband, my children, anybody, if I don't like myself? And if I'm so far from being a friend to anyone, then the whole superstructure of our lives (I being the hub) is faulty.

What I don't like is basic to our life. It begins way, way down. The befriender is sitting in judgment of the befriendee. The befriender does not like the innocent lies, the easy smiles, the easy faces, the cheerful greetings to people I neither respect nor understand. The befriender doesn't like the modus operandi of the befriendee, who toadies up to baby sitters, mothers-in-law, neighbors, teachers, butchers, cleaners, floor-waxing men, gas-station attendants. She not only listens but makes cheerful, helpful remarks. Invites them to tea. Drives them to the hairdresser if they're stuck. The befriendee spends half her life apologizing because it's raining, because the bananas aren't ripe, the melon too ripe, the shirts too starchy, the sweater too scratchy. Now they look to her for apologies even if there isn't anything to apologize for.

•

There are not mountains of fat. There are not even hills. Just enough fat to cloud the psyche. To keep me on the fence of whether to join the race or retreat, overblouse billowing behind me. Like the victims of anorexia nervosa, who starve themselves to an early grave or to a living grave because they have an irreparably distorted view of their bodies, I, too, am operating from a psyche that believes my backside could span the Grand Canyon.

Maybe it's being caught up in the farce that in order to give birth to eight- and nine-pound children you cannot have size 33 hips. It's frightening.

I read Ayds ads to psych myself up. In for the big dig. "I was the 320-pound baby of the family," says Martha Nick in her drab size 20 mantle. Martha had twelve fried eggs for breakfast, a pound of bacon, a package of buttermilk biscuits, a quarter pound of butter and a quart of milk. She really chowed down. Couldn't get a job because she literally didn't fit into a good many offices, so she stayed home and ate herself into an acute gall bladder attack. The surgeon wouldn't operate and, as Martha turned to leave, he grabbed her belly and said, "Get that off or you won't live six months." (Maybe he was married to Tiny Alice, who had no belly to grab.) So Martha ate less and took up sky-diving (no jokes about the Goodyear blimp, please). Today, at 145, she's come out of her shell, has a job with the telephone company and a steady boyfriend. "Marriage can wait," says Martha.

Then there was Janie Goff, who was her husband's warmth in winter, his shade in summer. But now that she's 82 pounds thinner, he's had to buy an electric blanket.

And how will I be thin? More authoritative? Will I stop asking everyone around me if they love me? Yes, I do ask that. I ask it in sneaky ways of the children. "Would you like another Daddy?" "Oh, no," they all squeal with complete conviction. "We always want to keep him." "What about another Mommy?" Suddenly they're engrossed in digging into their ice cups or tying their shoes, and the question is an intrusion. "Mo-o-ommm, you keep interrupting." Selective hearing they call it. Nick is always ready to answer in his uncomplicated way, "Mom, I like you." No matter what I ask him, he answers, "Mom, I like you." He doesn't want to commit himself to big, long-term answers, but he wants to reassure me as much as he can.

I've been working on attacking Daddy love first, because, in my eyes, my thighs are the neediest. I've been going down into my thighs to see what's up. First, I quiet my thoughts and think only of relaxing my muscles. I find I can relax my entire body by making sure the face muscles are relaxed. Also, when I'm completely relaxed, my mouth hangs loose, like that of a child who is concentrating. Without anxiety, I direct myself to enter a deeper state of relaxation, bypassing my ordinary mind—the mind that makes grocery lists, reads recipes.

Suddenly, I'm there. How do I know? By the way I see. Images come, as if on a large TV screen or just in the air, and I can control them. The trend of thought is associative rather than consecutive, as in real life. I try to recreate myself thin up on the screen. Not an ideal picture of Joey Heatherton or Charo, but me with my own physique. After half a dozen tries, I find I cannot recreate myself, thin or otherwise. As I construct one part, another disappears or becomes distorted or fades and drifts out of view. What do I know of my face and how I look? I've only known my face to paint it; I have not recently looked into my eyes in search of expression, emotion or recognition. The grocer knows my features more intimately. "Oh, yes," he will say if pressed with a modest description. "I know that woman. She comes in with small children and sometimes alone. Very friendly. Very nice."

I picture myself resisting food. Deliberately setting down a place to eat, selecting what to eat with a clear mind and a subdued heart rate. Normally, my eating patterns are agitated and intractable. Erotic, erratic and elusive. I cannot recount my eating habits with accuracy. When I am about to eat, a stranger inhabits my body and clouds my mind. It's the shadow. The shadow is doing the eating, and only he knows.

Today, something—an urge—guides my hands to my hips.

I feel a bone. I feel a muscle. I am losing inches from my hips. I am madly in love with a small bone or muscle or something hard that stretches from the upper back part of my thigh to my rear. It is the most beautiful thing I have ever felt and shows me what pleasures lie in store for the woman who loves her body. My neck is thinning out. It is gaining character, with lovely, thin ligaments, fragile bones in relief giving it planes and shadows. The neck. The calling card of the soul. The neck tells what you are. Fat and creased. Long and sinewy. Smooth and characterless. My saddlebags are also diminishing—those robust intruders carelessly added to my upper thighs by a sleepy Master Builder tiring of creation.

When I become properly thin, shall I consider attracting another man? See, that's my first thought. Irony, irony, thy name is life. I'm getting thin to put myself in another situation where the tacit and implicit provisos are that I will get fat and sad again.

I am going to continue to assume that everything is right with my world. I'm going to assume that I'm more than this two-dimensional creature torn between the pot roast and the brisket of beef. More than the feeling of wanting to create an ambiance around me that feeds my ego, an ego carefully superimposed and constructed over my lovely, unmuddled spirit by messages that have been pumped into my brain since time immemorial. Certainly in the vanguard are the messages of the last fifty years or so, but there are zillion-year-old messages as well. Soft skin is nice, and lustrous hair that falls softly and looks as if nothing difficult were ever done to keep it that way. A ready wit, even a cynical one, as long as it doesn't defile the sacred trusts—motherhood, an unselfconscious yielding in the bedroom, firm thighs, clear eyes, a clean bathroom, fresh flowers.

There's another dimension to me. I'm going to assume there's a more substantial me that is impervious to who loves me or finds me sexy. So much of what I think of myself is tied to that. If I'm thin and gorgeous, I can walk into a room with head held high, words tripping out with relaxed good humor. I can be kind and enjoy sunsets and walk in the rain and chat up the garbage man and the cleaning lady. Also, I am tied to my emotional possessions. I am my husband's income, his lean muscular body, his lack of a five-o'clock shadow. I am his ability to sail, his interest in birds as well as the stock market. Because he's well-rounded and well-to-do, I can snuggle in bed in the morning and say slightly irresponsible things at luncheons with the girls or large cocktail parties. My identity, my security, is as ephemeral as his next breath and his monogamous instinct. One heartbeat away from utter dissolution.

I'm sure there is more to me, and I'm banking on its emergence any day now, as, when you do stone rubbings, the harder you rub and the longer, the more complete a picture emerges.

Chapter Eight

SOMETIME AFTER 3 P.M., habitually a time to reassess the day, strive for renewed purpose.

I feel very strong now (they're all in my power), relaxed, too. There's no immediate need to do anything vengeful, but still some of the other, a small knot, is beginning to form at the base of my abdomen, where I mistakenly believe my stomach begins or ends. Andrew will burst through the door any moment and I will have to tell him . . . no! he will remember . . . that he has a violin lesson today and will lounge on the stairs, kicking the wall with oversized sneakers, arguing over that or something else; he is better at baiting me than I am at overpowering him with my size and knowlegde, this child.

The house is swaddled in a silence that is no longer welcome. It's unnerving. A long silence turns quickly eerie here. They're dead, I think, but I won't look just yet. Then I carefully itemize what I was doing at the time the thought of disaster hit me. When I calm down and can bear to talk about it, I'll tell anyone who will listen: I was shelling peas and thinking about Pauline Press, an old friend from boarding school, who was caught in bed with Lilly Medaglia (nothing much going on, just huddled together). Suddenly, I usher out Pauline and Lilly in thin nighties with thin arms and legs wrapped around each other and usher in dead babies. Dead babies at the bottom of the tub, under wheels of cars, under weighty pillows. "That's what it was, all right," I will say, "they were dead." It's dreadful. I have learned to live with dread, as perhaps I am meant to, part of the evolutionary vanguard where dread of the unknown (or the known) is taking a larger part in life in order to be eradicated altogether. It's coming to the fore in order to fade into the background, as in the cinematic device (corny) that shows the passage of years.

I should not entertain such images. It'll happen. Instead I should be entertaining sexual fantasies. Supplant the dead babies, a shivering Lilly and Pauline, with images of D. and me making love. I should be thinking cleverly about how I want him to do it to me so I have something concrete to tell him at night when he asks. He has not asked directly or insistently but there are hints. His desire for me is frightening. I have a generous, uncomplaining lover at my beck and call, but, still, there are gossamer innuendoes (concerning me) to be dispelled. I'm not sure I deserve them. I think there's a simple and logical explanation for my quixotic sexual dawdling.

●

Joshua is gone. Picked up by Libby, sleeping as he was left, not knowing where he'd been, eyelids fluttering but never opening. Maybe he'd rather not know. It occurs to me that Joshua has spent most of his two and a half years sleeping. I have seldom seen him awake. He has a sweet nature, however, and seems to have his father's metabolism, just as my second child is patterned more like the father and the first like the mother.

I called the Kennerlys again, thinking to outwit myself and the big icy block over Saturday's dinner, and surprisingly she was home and answered on the first ring. I took it as an omen and—instead of asking about a bread recipe (carrot bread), which I had planned to do while getting the feel of the conversation—I asked her right out to come to dinner.

She said they were free, surprisingly, and would love to come and wasn't it a nice surprise for an otherwise humdrum Tuesday. Half an hour later, surprise, surprise, I called back and left word with her daughter (thank goodness) that something had come up and we couldn't make it. I'm free again. The truth was stretched and I'm not yet enmeshed. Something *could* come up. D. doesn't ever lie (although he will reluctantly go along with my lies), but, then again, he seldom answers the telephone, where most of the lying gets done.

A detached but interested reviewer of life scripts might point out to me now that the choice of whether or not I join the race and lead an orderly life is no longer mine. I may be incapable of participating in, let alone initiating, the most simple social interaction. That I've lost my touch (or my marbles). I know there are certain things I do that are no longer sane. There is no order to my thoughts; they skip and dance from one subject to the next, a dust storm of free association, and my body follows suit. I skip and dart over the house, leaving chores half-done, empty pots to burn on the range, socks half-folded, children half-dressed, beds half-made. I blame it on the telephone's ringing or on the children, in need of any ready and believable alibi. But in truth, I am keeping myself tangentially tied to a vicious circle of disorder. A disorderly schedule in a disorderly house in a disorderly universe. Instead of sitting down to an orderly lunch, I plant myself at the open refrigerator, gobbling up tasty leftovers, gouging a piece of reluctant cheese, digging out a stubborn olive, downing appetizers and desserts, leftover sodas and half-eaten sandwiches in unacceptable order.

Sandy Rose's house is a bigger mess than mine, but Sandy does not read the chaos, the crispy crunches underfoot, as a direct statement of her inner turmoil nor does it impair her ability to compartmentalize and plan for her future. She can skip off to her Friends of the Earth meeting or her Food Co-op cashiering stint with zero guilt.

I asked her once if she used the time when her children were asleep or at school to clean her house.

"Rarely," she answered. "I feel that I'm entitled to that time for myself. They usually are gone three hours, and I won't say that I do nothing for three hours but enjoy myself. I do things like laundry or vacuuming but nothing major. I rarely do anything major. I feel little interest or involvement with my house. What I would like, if I could envision myself as a different person, I would like to really love my house and want to fix it up. Then I would use that time to do it."

"But you don't want to fix it up?"

"No. I want someone else to like it and fix it up. I would like it to look better but it wouldn't be a big kick for me if it did. I wish it were, for Dave's sake. He *does* wish it looked better."

"Does he get angry about it and tell you?"

"All the time."

"And how do you answer him?"

"I tell him I'm not very good at it and it's too bad for him that I'm that way but there's nothing much to be done about it." Here's one more woman, a sleek object hurtling in space to God knows where.

There goes poor Dave Rose, wiping his shoes when he leaves the house instead of when he enters. Spending more and more time at his frozen food publishing empire dreaming up articles entitled "Frozen New Zealand Lamb—Newest Thorn in the Side of the Lagging American Lamb Council" and, in between, thinking how he'd like to quick-freeze Sandy and reorder her molecules to make her more tidy or, at least, get her to admit it's wrong to accept such wanton disorder.

D., on the other hand, has never indicated the disorder handicaps him or his ability to enjoy his life in any way. He never mentions it. When I think it's getting out of hand, I mention it to him.

"Why don't you tell me to clean up this fucking mess?" I will ask him, eager for a strong reaction.

"Don't talk that way. Why do you have to talk that way?"

"Don't tell me how to talk."

At one of the meetings with the mystic, I found myself blurting out, "My house is a mess. Chaos. More out of its place than in it." "The house is you," replied the same man who had told me I didn't drink enough water. He didn't even turn to face me. His accusations don't anger me. There seems to be good reason to stash them away as solid truth. However, they are stunning. Like a stunning, unlooked-for blow.

I'm sitting on the oak stairs waiting for my kid to come home, facing my front door, which is just a brown rectangle surrounded by big sheets of glass. I've washed my face, put a little Erace around my eyes to make me appear rested (which it instantly does). You should be home when your kids come from school, they say. They should always find you there. No nasty surprises. Here are Andrew's steps now on the driveway, then a different echo as he rushes up the hexagonal pavers that lead to our front door. He's anxious to see me again, I suppose.

He always bursts in or else leans heavily on the bell, not waiting for us to answer. The smaller children and I are always startled by the bell no matter when it rings. We look at each other, stricken, and say, "It's the doorbell. Somebody at the door." We've been tricked. Nick usually trudges up the stairs, if he's awake, and assumes a put-upon air as he answers, to hide his excitement. Today, it's just me there, waiting when Andrew bursts in.

"Uh, hi." He immediately sits on the stairs and puts his fingers in his mouth, long legs now scrunched up to meet his elbows. There's a bit of awe I harbor for this strong-bodied, perfectly proportioned child. His hair falls into careless ringlets (which he hates; he wants the flat hair and tame look of his friend James). His face looks polished and flushed from exertion. He's been out in the world and I'm impressed.

"How was it today?"

"Aw . . . some good," fingers in and out quickly, "some bad."

"Mostly good or mostly bad?"

"The same for both."

"What was the bad?"

"Dopey George."

"Did what?"

"He always does bad things to me."

"Like what?"

"He holds my head close to the ground. Sometimes he bends my fingers back." Knowing eyes search my face for reaction.

"Why don't you stay away from him?"

"I like him. And I've got a good plan to get him to be my friend."

"What do you mean?"

"I'll be the one who acts droopy and then he'll want to know all about me."

"But when he wants to play with you, will you continue being droopy?"

"Oh, no! Mo-o-mmm." He's sure I'm teasing him. "I'll play with him."

I recognize his droopy, hard-to-get game as one I've played myself at times with a different twist. I have this little secret deep inside that I'm separated from him, D., and them. They're on one side of this great divide and I on the other. I have to keep certain things from them, beguile them in a certain way, distract their attention from my real motives. When we walk, I lag back, surveying them all.

It isn't an intentional something I've nurtured and decided on. It's an attitude that's grown and hardened. There's this distance and it could be just a smidgen of myself I'm saving without identity to whip out when all those other roles desert me—my hedge fund.

I think D. is beginning to suspect this is so. He no longer

looks at the *Côtelettes d'Agneau Ménagère* with such awe and gratitude. He now allows that the colossal dinners are diversionary. I just discovered it myself. I'm beguiling them, but he's onto something. (The children always knew.) He eats less and less these days. Small helpings. No second portions. He still gobbles down apple pie (his favorite), but soon he will see through that, too. I don't know how he realizes things and with what internal consequences (how it hits him). I don't know that much about him. I've seen him cry twice and, by his own admission, he "choked up" when he saw Amanda being born.

I relive that birth more than the others, going back to it again and again with relish and attention. Not for the birth —that went quickly and I couldn't see much—but for his reaction—a raw, simple and frightening emotion. I had asked him at the time how he felt seeing her born, and he answered, "I choked up." Now, I ask him over and over to describe what happened, just so I can hear him say once again, "I choked up." I didn't choke up. Exhilarated? Yes. Charged up? Yes. But I didn't choke up.

We all choked up when Nick went on the school bus to camp the first time. "Dry tears," Andrew called it when I pumped him for information. "He looked so dumb with his eyes so open. His bare legs showed under his raincoat, he looked like a two-inch mutt. It made me feel sorry for him. I know I hate him," he finished, mystified by his reaction.

But now I remember something D. said. Something that was said and quickly forgotten. He said, "I will be nice and like you right to the end, and the end, when it comes, will be a shock to you." I think that was on another night, or the day after another night, when we were more in control of our emotions and had some time to think. Another non-lovemaking night when he came out in his pajamas, which was a small surprise in itself; I seldom see him in his pajamas, he always seems to be dressed.

I was very busy in the sewing/laundry/project room and he asked me if I would like to jog with him in the morning and advised me to decide right then and there because it was too difficult to decide in the morning.

"No," I replied. "I don't want to do anything until I'm really ready to act and then I'll concentrate and have some sort of stepped-up program."

Then a few minutes later he came into the room, still pulling on his pajamas, and he said, "Does not doing anything include not making love?"

"Huh?"

"Well, I want to know where I stand. I'm not talking about tonight"—I suspect he was—"but I'm a married man and I want to know where I stand."

"I don't know where you stand," I said helplessly. I knew where he stood, but it was against my best interests to tell him at the moment. Anyway, it wouldn't have sounded coherent. I'm in such a tight, locked circle nothing else exists for me except my head. I'm trying to desensitize myself to my immediate surroundings and create a new and solid structure inside, built on what I want and on other possibilities. This takes time. A long, long time. Should I have told him, as Emerson said, that we're not done being created? That I've taken over my own creation?

The next night, however, I made sure I was in bed, smelling good and available. I didn't like that crack about his liking me and being nice right up to the end.

There was an incident recently that ties up with all this. One of my baby sitters, an older woman with grown children, was discussing the breakup of her son's marriage and shrugged it off. "My daughter-in-law simply did not like being married."

"What does that mean? She didn't like sex?" I asked.

"Yes. She didn't like sex." I suspected that wouldn't have been her answer had I not phrased the question, but it probably was the right answer. That is not the case with me. I remember being practically insatiable during our delayed honeymoon in Spain. Maybe it was all those electric Latin libidos sending out lust waves.

My ears perk up on hearing the news that someone does not like being married and knows it and can say it simply. It conjures up . . . what? Someone closed up tight for the season. A summer resort in the dead of winter. Desolate. Uninhabited. Myself. My own inner landscape. Not being part of a thriving, kicking, loving, apple-pie family still, to me, appears a cutting of the life line. But what is to be done? If, as Erving Goffman, the sociologist, anthropologist, breaker of shocking news, tells us, our whole business here is the fabrication of identity, then I've momentarily left the factory, closed down the loom, shut down the plant.

I think I've been fighting a headache for three straight days. It's hovering there, my old friend, the headache. I don't want to have a headache because I don't want to have to tell D. I have a headache. He will say, "Oh, no. Why?" as if I've betrayed him. There he is innocently eating his Steak Roquefort and I'm secretly harboring a headache. I run inside sometimes in the middle of dinner and put a rag around my forehead, Indian fashion, to hold my head together. I can't stand the slightest wobble. If I'm wearing a torn arm of one of his long-ago-favorite shirts, slate gray with white stripes, he will say, "I like your rag," trying to coax me into good humor. But it hurts to look up. He asks again why I keep getting headaches. "Either you're very sick," he surmises to himself, "or you don't want to face something."

Here is Andrew facing me—or rather not facing me but showing his determined back and set shoulders. I have given up trying to order his social life, which daily grows less promising, and I no longer feel a responsibility to decipher his true worries. He has his own strange priorities. When he was in first grade, he came home from school one day and announced with pride, "I went to the bathroom in school today."

"What?" I was shocked. It was December and he had been in school since September. "You've never used the toilet in school before?"

"No."

"But why?"

"It has a space in the middle. It's not like ours at all. And the water comes in very strong and makes a loud noise."

After that his grades improved. He began going to school cheerfully or almost cheerfully. He refrained from total cheerfulness in order to maintain some control over me.

"Suppose we couldn't bend our knees or our arms," he announces suddenly, rising stiffly. "We'd walk like this." He walks robot fashion. "Suppose we couldn't bend our hair. We couldn't get the ticks out. Our hair would be like a block of ice."

"Have you been talking about your body in school?"

"No,'" he says, in his knowing way. He tells me he's just been thinking about his body and all the wonderful things it does and did I know that an apple was nature's toothbrush. He knows why I ask him questions and what I really want to know and he nonchalantly steers me here, there everywhere but where I really want to go. Right now, it's apparent, he is fearing rigidity. Their lives are so rigid for their age. So civilized. He is already wary of rigidity and idolizing flexibility. As am I.

"We have a violin lesson today," I say. "The group lesson."

"I know." It's a weary, resigned voice and, while it produces the expected stitch of guilt, it also mobilizes me to act quickly and use his mellow mood to advantage.

I can't explain why a good mood starts sometimes. Why we're suddenly on the plus side of our natures and feelings. I have sent Nick in to wake Amanda, not wishing to face her annoyance (all day I'm dodging ill will. Should I face it like a man?), but she's padding down the cool oak floor, chattering away good-naturedly.

"Are we going to violin? Are we going to violin?" She pronounces it "bylin." Mesmerized by her cuteness, the boys now start to join her baby talk.

"Mada, Mada," says Nick, "we're going to bylin. Does Mada wanna go?"

"Yah," she squeals.

"Mada, Mada, Ady's home," says Andrew, no longer sullen and watchful.

They're all giggling and sucking in their breath and jumping gracelessly, performing for each other. They're so fresh with sleep, so rosy and moist. Their cells must be multiplying madly, like a speeded-up film. They're mad with livingness and could go mad with joy if I gave the cue.

There. You see. There's nothing at work here but an emotional malcontent pulled this way and that by a lunatic moon, taking her next of kin with her as she goes. My mood is their mood. My laughter triggers their deeper laughter. I have incorporated them into my soul in a frozen state of possibility, allowing them only as much life as I am capable of living. They play the same scene over and over, depending on me to liberate them. Well, I might. And I might not. Or I might do it piecemeal and then pull them back again so they'll never be whole.

What I choose for them will follow them the rest of their lives and show up again and again in future generations like an overbite, thick curly hair, an ability to draw, a fondness for chili peppers. They should be allowed more freedom. To unstuff pillows. Jump on mattresses until springs pop. Decapitate dolls. Unscrew screws. Unbolt bolts. Push Playdoh through the garlic press. Crumble toast. Smear applesauce. They say that in prehistoric times the infant held onto his mother's hair night and day (women had long, strong hair then), and that was his security. The infant never left his mother's side. What have I traded them for my nearness and is it a rip-off?

I could, right now as they're wiggling and giggling, reduce them all to tears with an over-the-shoulder remark. I could, given an additional few minutes, psych them out for a lifetime with a remark that carries the proper emotional punch. I am so devious, so congenitally Machiavellian that I surprise and scare myself. With seeming innocence, I could do such a thorough job on them, we'd all be candidates for a "Guinness Book of Weirdos."

> Dear Dr. Franzblau:
> My son is not doing so well in school. His mind wanders and he can't seem to concentrate on any subject for long. He was always a good student, polite and well behaved. But all of a sudden, he just stares into space for long periods of time and we can't seem to get through to him. Oh, yes, he also sleeps with me when my husband is on long business trips, which is most of the time. Can you help?

I know, for instance, that Andrew is impressed with and retains what I tell him because once, when I slapped him hard across the face, surprising myself as well as him, he advised me in a shaky voice that that was the worst thing you could do to a person. When I asked who told him that, he said I had, at a time when he had slapped his brother across the face.

Andrew also pointed out to me one evening that his pajamas were flammable (he pronounced it flaymable), it said so right across the label, and he was mystified as to why I would buy him flammable pajamas. Once when we had been driving behind a huge oil truck and he was jumping around on the seat beside me bumping my arm, I burst into tears and pulled over to the side of the road, saying we would all be killed and blown up because the truck was filled with gasoline, which is very flammable, meaning it can catch fire easily.

"Don't bite my arm," the baby sputters with mock bravado knowing full well I could bite her arm off if I so chose. "I am, too, going," says Nick, hugging the ground. But even as he says it, his voice cracks. What can he do if I decide to pick him up and contain him? I have all the options.

I can tie him in a closet. Keep him prisoner in a dark room (literally or figuratively). Make him sit on the toilet until his intestines begin to ooze out of his round pink fanny. Tell him gorillas are coming to get him. Paint such vivid and professional word pictures of monsters and ghouls. Create such a devastating feeling of loneliness. Promise him tiger fests and bogy men and crocodile-infested moats from his crib to the bedroom door. Taunt him with his frailties until he becomes deranged.

The dumbest of us is completely capable of wrapping them around our little finger. Of calling the shots. The hand that rocks the cradle does rule the world. It has always fascinated me that Pablo Casals loved his mother so; but I never quite believed him.

We started violin lessons because we were bored and lonely each winter and needed some place to go in the gray, long afternoons. Andrew and I were the teacher's first pupils —she had just arrived from Michigan—and it didn't look promising. We kept at it. Amanda was an infant carried from place to place in a small box that snapped together to make a bed. Nick, barely walking, was left sleeping in the car sometimes while Andrew and I tinkered with our instruments.

Now we go to the lessons because, as I explain to anyone who will listen, it is good for him and will serve him well later. He will be able to console himself by making music. It's good for his small muscle development (chronically pointed out as a weak point on report cards—he doesn't write well). I don't know why I feel he will need consoling later but assume he will because the thing he could console himself with and the abundance of which would make his small or large muscle development inconsequential would be my love, which I'm not at all sure is there. There are conflicting signs.

I think about him; as I've said, I always fear they're dead. I fear also that they will be warped, I fear they'll fail *and* succeed. When I watch them sleeping at night, I am consumed with a desire to take them back into my womb. To feel a closeness. To devour them when they are contained in their "big boy" and "big girl" beds and not give them a chance to wake up and threaten me with their voracious appetites and needs. They're a different race—they're bigger, stronger, smarter, less fearful. At this tender age they smell out my frailties and could make short work of me if they weren't guided by love.

I don't fear Communism. The red peril, the yellow peril, the black peril—all the perils pale before the threat I feel from my children, who live right here and whom I see every day.

I'm sitting on the outside porch of the violin teacher's house. It's an old-fashioned wraparound porch with stairs leading to a medium-size lawn and the normal, busy street of a house in the heart of a village. Nick and Amanda are riding their Little Wheels up and down the driveway that runs alongside the house. There is something about living in the heart of a village that appeals to me, although D. would say the grass always looks greener on the other side. I wouldn't even mind a row house, a teeming neighborhood. The suburbs are getting me down.

My friend Meg Riddley would say it's the alienation you feel from your family, so much boring transference. If you felt close to your dear ones, you wouldn't be yearning for row houses, dwelling back to back, people haunch to haunch. I don't think that's all of it. You have to fight what the culture is shoving down your throat. A young inventor and his wife I know wanted to move to the Village of Huntington so he could bicycle to work and generally simplify their life. The wife called several real estate agents requesting a house in the heart of the village with a small, manageable yard.

"But why not consider Dix Hills or Thunder Down Estates?" purred voice after voice.

"We want a house in the village."

"My dear," began one agent solemnly, "is there a physical disability? Someone can't see . . . blind . . . a lost limb?"

"No. Nothing like that. We just don't want to get into the car every time we need a loaf of bread."

"Oh," she chirped happily, "a one-car family."

My own house would look terrific if I cleaned it up. Elegant. A real estate agent's dream property.

> Arch.'s own wdland retreat. Contemp. openness without cold look. Exq. maint. free ext. cedar/ fldstone/glass. 3 magnif. int. stone walls, 2 w/fplcs. Cust. dream kit w/dmbwtr., expected light, unexpected light. Exq. tile throughout, 3 cust. baths, 4 bdrms (brthtking mast. bdrm suite), liv/din rm with soaring ceil. Unique elec. heat, tree top deck, winter water view of pvt. beach. mrg. rts., golf rts., many cust. xtras. For the demanding family with taste and a love of the great outdoors. A house for all seasons.

Ha, ha. But the walls are crawling with anxiety, fear, resentment. Contemporary resentment without contemporary sexual mores. We're all prudes here, modest.

Andrew doesn't like our house. When I ask him why, he says there's nothing to do there. For myself, this little run-down porch appeals to me, and I'm quite content to sit here inspecting the violin teacher's azaleas, her ivy, looking for signs of spring. I feel a potent, healing calm for the moment. If I could remain forever like this, in transit, instead of having to settle down.

I don't have any handy solutions as yet. I still have to face D.—not his anger, but his measured concern for the texture of his life, his needs. Then, too, this shouldn't be just another day . . . if I lose this momentum . . . it's taken me months to gain this momentum. If I lose it now, who knows when I will pick it up again? On the other hand, I have responsibilities. The children. Four of us to be mobilized and I don't really believe I can manage the children. I don't even know where we could go or how to tell anyone we're leaving in a convincing manner. What do you say?

I can't steal away and wait for my inner self to speak. A solution has to be pieced together from what's at hand. Life goes on. Besides, I know by now that answers never come when you're waiting for them, a dumb but true rule of life, answers only come when you're looking the other way. They come on little cat's feet, as the poet says.

The mothers are beginning to drop their charges at the curb and continue on. One mother, an attractive black woman in her early thirties with whom I've had dealings, is approaching, ready to join me on the porch steps. She sits close to me, assuming an identical pose, but the effect is different. She is not looking for anything—calmness, a change of scene, solitude. She is in command of herself, the situation, her life, the universe. I don't know why I think of her this way, but I do. As I've said, we've had dealings. We have a friend in common, a painter of Southwestern themes who has stomach ailments.

She's wearing a colorful scarf tied back on her head, a cunning device to show off her face, which is extraordinary—a perfect oval of medium brown skin. Her eyes are deeply set, even with their folds, two lighted ellipses. Between each eye and its brow there's a plump mound, the *mons ophthalmica* she calls them, telling me that they can, if properly emphasized, make one beautiful. Her very adequate *mons ophthalmica* are brightly lit with iridescent sea green eyeshadow, but the rest of her face is her own—no makeup. Sporadically, she represents a cosmetics firm with specialties for the black woman. "Oh, C." She's immediately engrossed with me, my face, my looks, my innards. She sees right through my innards. "You've cut your hair. I like it." She arches back to survey me. "Hmph. I never would have thought you could look like that. I think there's a lot to you you're not dragging out. That nobody would suspect." She gives a sensuous snort.

I know she's manipulating me, but for what end? About a year ago, I had on false eyelashes and she said immediately, "C., they make you beautiful. You're a beauty now. What are you going to do with yourself?" As if my life could now take a sudden dramatic turn.

"Do with myself?"

"You're not going to spend the rest of your life baking pies," she laughed. "I bet you do make pies." I do. I earn my keep and theirs by making pies. But each pie is eaten and forgotten and, presto, you have to come up with another that will be inhaled as well, unless it gives someone a stomachache, and then it will be remembered in a harsh way, the pie and I being forever bound. Up until that moment, I thought that was just what I was going to keep on doing—making pies. It had not yet occurred to me that I had alternatives. Child rearing clouds the mind.

"It's easy for you to talk; your Peter's six and in school all day. Mine start staking their claims in the middle of the night. First it's the drinks of water, then the bad dreams. By six-thirty in the morning, it's all over for me."

"That won't last." She eyes me suspiciously. "Are you sure you're not dragging it out?" Why do I think she has wisdom stashed in every pore? She's just a woman, like myself. Without the shyness. Without the pleading squint. "You've got to be smart for yourself," she says, wagging her head. "If you had two glasses in the house and one was chipped and a guest came and needed a drink, which glass would you give to yourself?"

"The one with the chip."

"Aha. That's wrong. Take the perfect one and let the guest have the cracked one. Let the rest of the world have the cracked glass. After all, if you can't have the perfect glass in your own house, where are you going to have it?" It seems dumb to just agree with her, so I say nothing. "I went through the selflessness bit in my first marriage. My first husband was a white man and he kept our marriage a secret because his father was dying and was supposed to leave him fifty thousand dollars. He didn't care about hurting the old man; he just wanted the fifty thou. When the father died, he left the money to the mother. So I still stayed in the closet. Then the mother overdosed herself and left the money to a sister who moved to Europe and spent every penny. My husband cracked up after that but I didn't stay around to watch it. I just got the hell out of the closet."

I wondered if she meant literally in a closet or figuratively but remained silent. Now she's inspecting my close-cropped hair with an innocent, little girl smile on her lips. A part of me wants to be taken under her wing. Her confidence is mesmerizing, but now I remember she's always affected me like that. Once her brother showed up (very dark skinned) and I was confused and angry because I had completely forgotten she was black.

"Now that you have a new look, maybe the rest of you will come inching out. A whole new person." Oh, you're right, I think, but for the life of me I can't come up with an innovative fact about myself. Just the same old me lapping up her hints of my beauty, my unsuspected assets, my potential for a bold leap. Sometimes I feel a true beauty and believe the best of everything is mine. I walk differently, almost a glide. After all, you can't ignore D.'s craggy good looks, his large imposing head, our money, our children. I have crawled my way to a certain vantage point in society. If we've all been given a certain amount of funny money to parlay into our various life situations, I've got a bundle to play with. Am I going to throw the baby out with the bathwater over a few vague dissatisfactions?

But this is not what she has in mind for a new bold me. "You have to be smart for yourself." Manipulative pause. "My husband knows I have my own life separate from the life we lead together." She's sizing me up to see how much I can take. "I've never had trouble attracting men. I see them. Frank knows I see them. In my career it comes up and I can't just play little Mary Housewife. Nobody wants to know her or spend any time with her. You wouldn't either if you thought about it. I see other men and it doesn't necessarily end up with sex."

"Of course not." I thought it did.

"But sometimes it does. I used to see a guy and this did end up with sex, but it was too kinky for me. All he ever wanted to do was close his eyes and have me touch his penis with things . . . objects. He wanted to guess what they were . . . a comb, a glass, a pencil. Can you imagine . . . in a year, he never guessed anything . . . once, maybe, a begonia leaf. I was attracted to him for a while."

She's crazy. What is she suggesting? She sees through my troubles, there's no doubt about that, and while her solutions may not appeal to me, this wild woman gives me hope. I need some true craziness in my life instead of dull anger or civilized barbecues. You never know when a little inch of hope is going to sneak in, opening things up, parting the gelatin and dragging me out. A glimpse. A shadow behind a screen. A suggestion of what I could be—a lithe, forward-moving woman with carefree hair. Not an aping of her, but myself, free of my own one-track mind, a new soul doing things the old soul never considered. Thinking myself strong, not asking directions, like a child. Finally, growing up.

"Of course, I don't know what arrangement you and D. have . . ." Each sentence is a vat of implications.

I look down at my hands, clicking nails together. No arrangement at all. I'm interested to see if she will let me be.

She knows how to manipulate me. Once last winter she came with her husband and child for a visit. Their house was being painted, and the smell drove them out. In the middle of the evening she said, "Frank thinks you meant for us to stay the night," which forced me to say they could. She kept the possibility alive all evening to taunt me. But I only know that now. When she was doing it, I didn't know it, which is important because I would have hesitated and she would have stayed, just to prove she could.

She chose me wisely. I would have allowed that to happen to me because she is stronger than I. I'm trying to think, who am I stronger than? It's not nice to be manipulated and know it and not have enough energy to do anything about it. To have a kink in your metabolism.

If D. were different. If he were a suave, cigarette-lighting, door-holding, glib savant, would I be at another place in life, in another state of mind? I disdained so much when I was picking and choosing. This one was a clod, that one lacked taste, one was too loud, one too quiet, mousy, obvious. Now, look at me—a little cut-out doll accommodating the insurance companies. So interchangeable, living so removed from reality it wouldn't matter who was sitting opposite me at the dining table. (Except that the one who is sitting there does smile and try to soothe me.)

A little veil is parting. It seems a sad, cruel thing to continue this way. I know now that daily I have been saying quietly to myself, litany style, the way the nuns say their rosaries, I have been praying without ceasing about my leaving. I haven't said I'm leaving, but neither have I really committed myself to them, to D., to the life we're leading. I have my thumb forever out, waiting for a ride out of here. I'm here physically, but psychologically, emotionally, I pulled out a long time ago. If I never get my ride, madness will whisk me away. A diabolic madness that doesn't require confinement, that is not outwardly violent, that is not punishable by law.

I know some of that madness has begun because, although

I can make my face grim with anger to frighten the children, lately I have felt a facial grimace that was not of my doing . . . snap . . . it came about all of its own and there was terror in their faces and they kept giving me sly sideways glances as if I were a sick pet they expected to die.

Chapter Nine

5:15 NICK HAS FOOLED WITH THE CAR CLOCK. We haven't reached home yet, it couldn't be so late. It doesn't matter, the day is closing up.

Suppose I were to say to D. tonight, "D., I'm leaving," or "D., we have to make other arrangements." And suppose he answered, "Oh, going to the supermarket without the kids? Good idea." Or, "Arrangements? Can't the baby sitter make it?" before even realizing we weren't going anywhere.

If I told him after dinner, it would ruin the best part of my day and might come out slapstick, Abbott and Costello, Laurel and Hardy. Who's on first, etc., etc.

And how would I break it to the children? "By morning, I won't be here. Mommy's going away for a while."

"Forever?" Andrew would ask gleefully and force me to answer yes.

"Good," he would say. Nick would say "good," too, but then he'd say, "I want to go with you. You never take me anywhere." Amanda would say, "I want you, I want you," and attach herself to my legs.

I'm at my best after dinner. If you don't like the mornings, you don't like yourself. If you don't like the afternoons, you don't like your work. If you don't like the night, you don't like your life. I hate afternoons but do like the night, or part of the night.

The sudden awkward breaking of bad news. Finding the right time is as awkward as the news itself. I thought this problem out carefully last Thanksgiving. It must have been on my mind.

We were speeding up to Troy in D.'s Porsche to visit his sister. Outwitting the cops. Outwitting Watergate and all its aftermath—the gas shortage, the speed limit, the money shortage. With our two bottles of Gallo's varietal wines cooling in the trunk, we were invincible. "We brought you some wine," I'd say. "New varietal wines from Gallo. They're made from French grapes grown right in California." The vines were grafted, transported, nurtured. Put into like climate. A like rocky, sandy, stubborn, unyielding soil. In like horseshit. In like everything. The first varietal wines from the people who previously gave you just any old crap from a mixed bag of grapes. Long, slender, expensive-looking bottles for people with long, slender taste and intellects.

It makes a good yarn and perfect for the likes of me. Good old home-grown schnapps. Why make the French rich? Of course, all these implications would be lost on my sister-in-law, who had always been pro-American anyway and not taken in by French charm.

We were bouncing along at a gay, or almost gay, clip, me saying "Uh, oh" every time we came to a road sign. He said, "This is where we turn."

I said, "Uh, oh, this is where we get lost." We both laughed good-naturedly, or almost good-naturedly.

The car quickly becomes our shroud, sheltering us from daily life. While we're on the move, nothing can touch us. The environment becomes friendly. Hostility stops. Love blooms. We eat up the miles and gulp cleansing breaths that start us afresh. There must be unique healing that takes place in the car or perhaps it's a demilitarized zone, because, when we get out of it, we visibly and invisibly regroup our forces, steel ourselves, take stock of our armament. Again, we're entering the arena. We have to interact, behave some way toward each other, cope with the identities handed out to us by our loved ones. Tolerate opinions, suggestions, repetitions, banalities, wisecracks, and so on.

The next day, after our trip, over a dinner of pale, warmed-over turkey (a beast that had been 80 percent breast. A Jayne Mansfield of the gobble-gobble set. "What a breast on that bird," my father-in-law had said), we were enjoying those odd few moments when the children, tired of distracting us, had settled into their after-dinner quiet. He sat at the table, relaxed, while I bustled around cleaning up. (There is a ready language for housewives. I don't believe anyone else in the world bustles.) We both had the trip on our minds and it occurred to me to say, "The way you told your sister about Cynthia's death, I don't know why, but it sounded as if you were setting her up." I began thinking about the scene. How he had stood by the big picture window, hands in his back pockets, looking straight ahead. His words had been . . . well, he had set her up. He had said, "Erica, I've got something to tell you." Pause. Then quickly. "Cynthia died."

This had to be farce at its best and I began to laugh out of proportion, as I thought of it. I sputtered, lost my breath, my chest hurt. Big fat tears rolled down my cheeks and I held my hands over my face and turned away.

"Why turn away?" he said. "You can look at me and laugh." I could not.

Then he started talking about the day he heard his mother had died. A dirty trick, since I had to stop laughing. He was in a history class at college and someone came in from the administrative office to get him. "You've got a call. It's bad news." A stranger, someone he'd never seen, coming up to him and saying simply, "You've got a call. It's bad news."

"I had to go all the way across campus to the administration building to take the call." I was completely caught up in the tragedy of one's mother's dying suddenly, but then he told me that he had known the night before that she was critical and he had accepted then that she would die. To me, this was not the same and I lost interest. I was, at the moment, only interested in the sudden, awkward breaking of bad news.

There is no graceful way of saying, "I'm leaving you." How does one approach it? There is no moment that will present itself and say, "OK, now!" And the difference between saying it and not saying it is so great that it never gets said. Do we stay married, in dead-end jobs, in dead-end friendships, for lack of an opportunity to end them? When you have the momentum, the moment doesn't present itself. When the moment presents itself, the momentum isn't there. As for myself, when I say anything of great emotional importance, it's never taken as such. It must be the quality of my voice or the economy of words, or the choice of words.

"I want to become a nun," I once said to the mother superior at my school, having worked up the courage over a period of hours to enter her queer-smelling bedroom-office. She laughed and told me to go out and play.

"I love you," I once said to someone I really loved, and he told me I was the only person who could say "I love you" and make it sound as if I were scratching my knee at the same time. Actually, I have never heard anyone say "I love you" in an appealing way. Emotion distorts the voice, or else the reverence distorts the voice. Whatever . . . my beloved went away never believing me. If I had protested and asked him to please believe me, he would have believed me less. Or maybe he didn't want to believe me. I'm not even close to having the proper emotional hold on myself to say, "I'm leaving." And suppose no one understood what it was I was saying? Suppose the whole world's gone mad?

No, no, no. You can't approach it from the outside in. The mystic's right.

If I did tell D. anything decisive, the first words out of his mouth would be, "Oh, God. What now? What happened today? Was it such a bad day?" Men always think it's what happened today that's the problem. "Nothing now. No. Not a bad day at all as days go. A little dull. Very dull as a matter of fact. You know that shit they hand you about children being so fascinating to watch as they grow and change and mature just before your eyes. Well, it isn't true, or have I told you that before? I guess I've told you that before."

"Why do you have to use that language?"

"You always say I should make decisions when I'm calm," I continue, ignoring his last remark. "Well, I'm calm. See, I can focus my eyes and look right at you. Feel my pulse. Go ahead." He makes no move to touch me. "Look, if you can't take me seriously when I'm calm and you can't take me seriously when I'm agitated, when are you going to take me seriously?"

Jesus, it isn't only D. Nobody takes mothers seriously. The pediatrician doesn't. The pediatrician's nurse doesn't. She won't put you through. The obstetrician calls you a big girl or a good girl or a bad girl or just one of his girls. The internist doesn't take anyone seriously, so no offense there. The deli man doesn't take me seriously, he says, "Hi, Hon." Other women don't either. They say, "Oh, come on," when I say I'm afraid of the telephone (very frightened) and always feel defeated when I turn to it. Not only defeated—captured and bound.

The children are quiet as we ride home, swaying with the turns and twists of the road. I feel sorry for them when they're quiet.

"Who called you at the boys' club yesterday?" I ask Andrew by way of conversation. Andrew has just begun to go to the boys' club and yesterday was his second day. "Did they page you over the loudspeaker?"

"Uh? Oh, yes. They paged me . . . well, I don't know. One of the big boys came over, Paul. He told me to go upstairs."

"And who was on the phone?"

"My father." He says it reverentially.

"Were you so happy to hear from him?"

"Yes. I told him I had gotten my card and the color of it and what number I had . . . where it says No., which is an abbreviation for number. I knew I had something more exciting to tell him than that, but I couldn't think of it. And even when he picked me up on the way home I didn't think of it until after supper. The better, more exciting thing was that I had seen five trains go by."

"What is your number? Do you remember?"

"Oh, yes. I couldn't forget that. It's M-361."

I know who called him. He knows I know who called him, but it's a conversational gambit we have for reliving good times. "Where did we go today, Nicky? What did Nicky see at the Post Office today? What surprise was in the mailbox?" We make believe no one knows anything.

We're passing the Oyster Bay Community Hall, where Nick used to attend a playgroup last year, and Nick insists we drive up to the door.

"That's my school," he says in a throaty voice.

"Why don't you shut up about that school?" says Andrew. "It isn't even a school. Just a playgroup and you don't go anymore."

"Yes, I do. A bus is going to pick me up and take me there. A bus *does* pick me up and take me there."

"Liar. You lie all the time. No bus is going to pick you up. You lie all the time." He does. I don't know why Nick lies, but he enjoys it tremendously. Lies roll off his tongue with ease and satisfaction. He lies about silly things—his name, his age—and about complicated things—his dreams. Lies, lies, lies. I would say Nick was a happy and unmuddled child if he didn't concentrate so much on the past. He clings to it like a life preserver. Talks only of last summer's camp, last week's library book, which he wants to borrow again and again, last night's dinner, last month's ferry ride. He goes back to his past like a digger of wells or treasure holes looking for minutiae, nuances and deeper revelations.

He clings to memories of his old playgroup and notes the building with ecstasy and relief each time we pass it. Nostalgia is his beat. For instance, now, he is looking everywhere —in the supermarket, the playground, passing car windows, the shoe repair shop—for *Hildy*. Sweet Hildy, who, it turns out in his recollections, swam so well. Hildy, who, of all those fresh and upturned faces at camp, shone as his one star. When he finally calmed down long enough to think about it, Hildy was gone. But her presence is as real as ever and he reminisces with a sweet longing in his voice and eyes. It would be useless to remind him that he cried bitterly every time I left him at camp with sweet Hildy.

Andrew, on the other hand, can't stomach the past. It is yucky, undistinguished and filled with mortifications that he will not review for love or money. Any sentence that begins: "Do you remember the time we . . . ?" "Oh, yeah, yeah, yeah," he will respond impatiently with vacant eyes. Then he introduces a new subject or becomes deeply engrossed in retying his shoes.

Who are these charming strangers? These charming cannibals? Why think of them as mine? Who are these visiting firemen? At best, they're guests. "Would you treat a guest that way?" asks Haim Ginott. "Would you tell a guest who spilled his ice cream cone, 'You clumsy idiot. Look what you've done?' Certainly not. You would say, 'What a shame. Here, let me get you another.' "

They should be treated like guests. The guest room. The guest treatment. The relieved, bittersweet goodbye when it's time for them to go. Tell them you won't baby sit or loan them money. On the other hand, you won't beg them to call and will never say, "Long time no see," or "Hi, stranger," or "I see you're still alive." And when they ask how you are, you won't say, "I'm still breathing."

"When Nick is ten, I'll be . . ." begins Andrew.
"Thirteen."

"M-o-o-mmm, I wanted to figure it out."

"Figure out what you'll be when Nick is twenty."

"No. I only wanted to figure out just that one."

"I'm sorry."

"You're not sorry. You never let me do anything. You have to butt in."

Silence from me.

"I'm hot, let's go swimming at the Y tonight."

"We have to go home and cook supper."

"Wes go swimming. Wes go swimming," says Amanda.

"I want to go to the Y. I want to go to camp this day. I'm bored," says Nick.

"It's after five. We're going home to have supper."

"What's for supper? Another yucky thing I'll hate?" says Andrew. He's scrunched up in the front seat, feet braced against the dashboard, hands in his mouth or around his mouth.

"Boston scrod."

"Boston crud. Just like you. You're cruddy."

"I'm not cruddy." I'm sure he doesn't know what *cruddy* means.

"Every time I have a bad day, you make it worse. You tease me."

"How do I tease you?"

"By having this yucky dinner and then saying Boston scrod. You think that's going to make me interested because it sounds mysterious."

As a matter of fact, that's just what I do think. So why the hell isn't he interested? Why isn't he crawling with joy and laughter? I'm being inventive and patient and stuffing their vicious little bodies with protein. Giving them a full and varied day. Talking up instead of down. Keeping their chests inflated. Keeping everyone's chest inflated. Theirs. D.'s. The cleaning lady's. On the other hand, I seem to be bucking the trends in the house. When I'm cold, they're hot and, even though I allow for their hotness, they won't allow my coldness. Why this constant stream of hostility? Why do I always end up the shit, while D. and the children remain the unshit, like the Un-Cola.

Fortunately for both of us, he recognizes a boy on the road near our house.

"There's Johnny."

"Do you have any more fights with him on the way home?"

"No. He's on a different bus now. He's in the third grade. He's not even in the same school. He goes to the elementary school."

"You'll be there next year."

"Yes, but I've still got a whole year to go at the primary."

"Not really. Two thirds of the year are over."

"What's a third?"

"If you divide something into three equal parts, each part is a third."

"Is it half a quarter?"

"No. A quarter is one-fourth and a half of that is one-eighth."

"Is it half of a half?"

"No. Half of a half is one-quarter."

"Is a third somewhere between a half and a quarter?"

"Exactly."

"How'd we get on this subject anyway? What a dumb subject."

"You asked me what a third was."

"Before that."

"I said your school year was two-thirds over."

"Before that."

"We were talking about your being in the elementary school next year."

"Before that."

"We saw Johnny and I asked if you had any more fights with him."

"OK. There."

"Why did you want to know?"

"I just wanted to know where it started and how it ended up." Like an impatient dictator pumping information from his aide-de-camp, he insists I make sense of his world.

You can learn a lot from children, they say. If you're so inclined. If you're so in need. If you're so in luck. If you're so fucked up. You can learn that following a thought from beginning to end is tracing creation. Is tracing life to death, morning to night. But so what? If you know all this and prefer being beaten to being caressed, what have you got? Air. Atmosphere. Cotton candy. Give me a shallow, pampered woman and I'll show you a well-integrated person.

I don't trust wisdom anymore. The minute you're wise to something, it becomes obsolete and of no further practical use. It clutters and upholsters your mind and is utterly useless in solving daily problems. Wisdom in progress is a little better, ultimately more taxing and fickle. But if you've wrapped up an idea and know it well enough to relate it to another, it's nothing more than a conversational gambit and bears no resemblance to reality.

Which leads me to the ultimate scary question—how then do we help ourselves? How do I—a slightly plump, well-to-do housewife on the verge of discovering my madness, with three adorable children, verging on hyperkineticism, an adoring husband who goes on in the midst of it all daily setting his "Kant-Miss" mousetraps, catching a mouse a day even though we beg him to stop—map out a platform for living? What I took for me isn't me and what I'm finding out to be me won't tolerate about 80 percent of my present life.

The business of life, the mystic would say, is finding ever-novel solutions to synthetic problems. He is saying that we can create an image in thin air, so to speak, and, by some process that is inevitable, that imaginal scene, object, whatever, is breathed into life and becomes part of our conscious existence. Furthermore, it happens in such a normal, unspectacular way that we are tempted to shrug and say it would have happened anyway and forget we ever drew up the plans. After a while, though, you get wise to the whole process and see each demonstration as proof. The only prerequisite is to systematically enter into the feeling of your wish fulfilled by whatever method excites you. To participate in an imaginal drama at the moment you receive it. The more important outcome, however, is what happens to you inside. Subtly, as you pump new information into your psyche, the inner terrain takes on new contours. Aha. Every result brings more than you bargained for.

Lately, I'm scared to think about what I think I should think about, which is leaving. I'm afraid I will really leave. That if I don't leave D. will continue to think of me as he thinks of me and the children will continue their baiting games and I will continue my subversive activities.

D. knows a lot about me. But a lot depends on what he knows and in what order for it to make any sense. He can't help wanting me to fall into a pattern that will be to his advantage, even though he professes to be open to change. We have a gentlemen's agreement over how far to go in exploring each other. What good would it do to go further? You can easily prove anyone crazy, there's no point to that.

How *does* he view me? A charge, his charge? A person with limitations (where logic is concerned) who must have her bedclothes arranged around her, whose clutch must be inspected. He has to worry over my car, my health insurance, my feelings. He must view the possible hurt to my feelings as he views the possible hurts to my clutch. He often says, "I have to be so careful what I say to you." That's not quite true. He doesn't realize that it is the specific things he says with his specific knowledge of me that make for fireworks. He doesn't have to be *so* careful.

I must get a look on my face, a stance, something that makes him ask each time I have some grievance on my mind if I'm going "to start that again," but it occurs to me now that

I've never made him tell me what it is I am going to start. As a matter of fact, I myself don't know what it is he's talking about. Usually when he asks me if I'm going to "start that again," I go into a blind rage because I haven't really started anything, and it slips my mind to ask him what he means.

But I think I don't have to ask him because if I lay it all out, what he means is am I going to interfere with the low-frequency happy waves that are floating around him and shriek about how bored, depressed, burdened, glutted, vacant, hateful, indignant, revengeful, I feel. And, I am. It has already been established that I do not wish to suffer in silence. Why should I?

There is inequity here, and the pattern now is that I can't bring up anything without its being lumped indiscriminately in the "not starting that again" file. Who will help us break this cycle?

Sometimes when I'm choking with anger and wish to hurt him, there is a tiny voice that breaks through and says, "If you really want to change anything, change yourself. Take control of the anger, turn the feelings around. Wait for a saner time."

It's a funny thing about creation. It only happens when you manage a few seconds of unawareness. A solution comes when you're uncaring of a solution. The telephone rings when you stop listening. The water boils when you become interested in what's going on outside the kitchen window. Little solutions. Big solutions. It doesn't matter. All you have to do is manage a few seconds of unawareness, the mystic says, and creation is upon you. While it seems absurd for life to work this way, it is comforting to know that this is the way it will always be.

If I don't start living at a more realistic level, I will never live at all. I need a philosophy of life. Yes, that's it. A working philosophy instead of just seesawing sloppily all over the place, working out a new and separate ethic for every event that perplexes me. I have to stop living as if I have an entire lifetime left. To begin taking my life seriously.

Once D. went away. We took D. to the airport and the goodbye was rushed because he was anxious for me to take the right road out of the airport and a uniformed man was hurrying the cars through. I looked back through the side window and tried to wave, but he's a tall man and his head was well out of view. The children weren't happy to be cheated out of watching the planes and I felt very much like giving in to them since it would just be the four of us together. I was also glad to see the proper road home and looked forward to an unhurried breakfast and the Sunday papers.

Unlike many men I know, he had never traveled on business before, and we're a close-knit family. That's how we would be described if we gave out the details of our life to someone who wanted to sum it all up. We always take the children with us on vacation. D. always went with me for their checkups when they were infants. The pediatrician, completely confused by the appearance of a father, spoke exclusively to him.

When he went up on that plane he disappeared into thin air and I couldn't reconstruct him, in the air or anywhere. His absence those first few hours was frightening. The sense was of a huge padded cell that absorbs all noise, the children's chatter, my conversation. He had taken more than one person's presence away from our house and it was a sad and disoriented group that was left behind. We seemed less capable than before and not content with each other.

He warned me I'd be sad. He said he was better at imagining how things would be than I was. He had been sad all week and was sure I'd be surprised by my own feelings at the last minute, the way it happened when Andrew started school and I burst into unexpected tears when he boarded the bus. I had been so eager for him to go.

Chapter Ten

TIME OUT.

There was a strange telephone call today, which I hesitate to mention, fearing it will carry undue importance. It could easily throw everything off. To do what I'm doing, which is trying to make a coherent decision about my life, I need an absolutely clear mind and conscience. If a child is ill, all bets are off. If a car is smashed . . . well. The call was from my mother.

My mother has complained to me in times past that I treat her like a dog. She says, "You treat me like a dog." Or maybe she says I treat her worse than a dog. Either way it's a poor simile. I've never had a dog and neither has she. What's more, no one has strong feelings about a dog (certainly not on the negative side, which is the side that interests her), and I do have very strong feelings about my mother and she about me. But I'm stumped as to what it is we want from each other.

She wants power over me. She has slipped and said so right out. "If I hadn't left you with your father, I would have some power over you." This is not a healthy goal but she wouldn't see it that way. I couldn't say, "Mother, it isn't healthy for you to want power over me or any other human being."

When I try to smooth out the junked-up reasoning, what I come up with is that she wants power over me so that I may provide her with some emotional kicks. She wants me to give her what she cannot give herself, I suppose, which is solace, comfort, nurturing, obedience, a sense of power. She wants me to nurture her single-handedly.

For myself, my desires from her are simple. I want her to do all my shitwork with a smile on her face and a gladness in her heart and ask for nothing in return. Clearly, we both must compromise.

When I think about my mother at the time that she was properly and rightly my mother, mentor, etc., I think of a beautiful and popular divorcee. I was a child of five or six, the only survivor of numerous pregnancies (the exact number of which I had to take on faith). She was a beauty without the features of a beauty—thin lips, arched, penciled brows, small eyes. Her skin was very white. Mine is darker and my features are all my father's—large eyes, short nose, childish lips.

Her married life was desperate, to hear her tell it. She miscarried everything—boys, girls, twins—she couldn't tolerate being pregnant. Couldn't eat a bite. Couldn't sleep a wink. Vomited daily, hourly. When she did make it to term, the children entered the world without enthusiasm, hardly stirring. I, myself, according to my mother, stubbornly refused food and drink for a week. Wouldn't cry. My stubbornness at birth set the tone for our relationship and it never improved. I've been bucking her ever since.

She claims to have all or part of her liver out, although I don't believe it's possible to live without a liver or part of a liver. I could easily find out and confront her, but then I would have to find out other things and confront her with those as well. Why she left my father. Why she gave me up. Why she was, for instance, so undesirable, mean, shitty, whatever, that she drove my darling Daddy away. Or did I drive him away with my magical thinking?

What I feel for my mother is inextricable from what I feel for D. and the children, and I won't be able to solve one satisfactorily without solving the other, but I've delayed solving the other for such a long time and I don't presume to have the energy to deal with it now.

Why not live and die without solving it? Anesthetized. There's plenty to do.

I may have it all wrong. The dilemma I share with my mother may have nothing to do with the dilemma I share with D. and the children, but if I'm convinced it does—it does. Better deconvince myself *or* solve it.

The call was mysterious because we have not been in contact with each other for a year (her decision—had her phone changed and then, not a word except for a garbled telegram to Andrew on his birthday, sent from Connecticut, where she does not live).

I don't think she cares much for D. She's crazy. D.'s a mother's dream, but, of course, he further blocks her power drive.

Obviously, my mother's wrong about the lack of power she has over me. She has great power over me. That's precisely why I feel so threatened and thrown off by this telephone call. I would not be surprised by anything my mother did, natural or supernatural. After all, she's my mother. I think she's crazy enough to do anything, desperate. *Or*, she has made me crazy enough to believe she'd do anything.

These are some things (by no means a complete list) I'm crazy enough to believe about my mother:

That she's working on me in some mysterious, secret way to ruin my marriage.

That she may have unhealthy interest in my children and wish to woo them away from me because of all her unfulfilled pregnancies (plus, she's bored).

That she has the power to have weird things happen in our lives so we will, in the end (or the middle), come running to her.

That I will ultimately, no matter how hard I try, think,

meditate, get analyzed, end up exactly like her—husband gone, children scattered to the winds. What's more, I will be the author of that tawdry script.

Perhaps she stopped sleeping with my father the way I'm easing out of sleeping with D., and that's why he left her, although she always claims to have left him.

"OK, Doctor, help me out. Do I want to leave D. because my mother left my father?"

"Do you?"

"I don't know. I asked you first."

"What do you think?"

"Sometimes, I think I do. And sometimes I think I don't. That it's my own good idea because marriage is suffocating, non-growth-promoting and a cop-out, no matter how terrific the husband. It has to come to no good."

"Why do you think you want to do what your mother did?"

"To show her I love her."

"But you don't love her."

"True. But I want to get her off my back and my conscience. I want to do something that I think will please her to make up for not loving her. If I end up just like her, won't that please her? Imitation is a form of love." A quick image of me, alone, playing power games with my children, telling lies about my liver or lack of a liver, reliving each pregnancy, vomit by vomit, forgetting that I sailed through my pregnancies like Cleopatra on her barge, never looking better (except for a suspicious brown line that divided my torso in two, extending from cervix to breastbone. A misplaced mask of pregnancy?).

"Why don't you try just loving her instead and forget about imitating her?"

"You mean if I love her I won't be forced to imitate her?"

"Right."

"How do I do that?"

"That's for me to know and for you to find out."

•

When Mom and I did live together in those early years, our *angst* and troubles and travels were a miniparable. We traveled to Mexico, where she ran a boarding house. She was an entrepreneur, my Mommy was. I spent most of my time playing hooky from the American school and sank lower and lower into precocity, tap dancing and such. When she ran a dressmaker's shop, I became a great little sewer. Finally, when it was time to take school seriously, we got on a bus and traveled to Washington, D.C., through Texas, a long and adventuresome trip that instilled in me the love of being in transit. In D.C., I was deposited with my rich father and his four bachelor brothers. After that, my relationship with my mother was sporadic, but in no way did that weaken her hold over me.

No human on earth can set me up like my mother. (Andrew comes close.) She can create a dread in the pit of my stomach that travels up fast and furiously with a simple remark. She wants to have "a little talk with me." What the hell does she want to talk about?

She wants to grab part of my life, slice me up bit by bit and lock me away in some needy corner of her. She'll tuck me in her head, under her armpits, in her stomach, her heart, her ears. She's going to use me up bit by bit, all on herself. There'll be nothing left.

And if I refuse. If I say, "Go to hell. There's not going to be any little talks or big talks, tell me right now what you want and don't leave me wondering and afraid, you crazy bitch," then, of course, she'll be angry and won't speak except to quite correctly call me unreasonable and a little crazy. Why would a sane person react so violently to her mother's simply saying, "let's have a little talk"?

There's nothing to talk about. I don't want there to be anything to talk about. Ever. I'm afraid of what she'll finally tell me, or ask of me, or do to me, or not do to me. Who knows?

Of course, my mother doesn't really want to slice me up bit by bit. She's just very good at making me believe that's what she wants to do. Or worse. Actually, I feel she wants to do something worse, something even more threatening and longer lasting, but I can't imagine what. I use the "slicing up bit, by bit" image because that's as far as my imagination goes. Deep down, I think it's worse.

If I could forget her existence, there would be no problem. However, I think of her. Even now, though we've moved since she saw us and it's hard to find our house, I think she knows all about us. She knows exactly what we're doing and what we're feeling and she knows all my business—that my thoughts run crazy at certain times of the day. As my desire to fight and work for my marriage ebbs, a smile of satisfaction spreads over her too-full face. Strangely, even though she's now in her sixties, her face remains unlined. It's a smooth, uncluttered face and I wonder if lack of living does that to you. Maybe her brain is shriveled and wizened instead of her face. My own face is smooth. I don't look my age.

Enough of this eeriness, there are loads of people who love my mother. Scattered throughout New York, there are dozens of receptionists, parish priests, lonely widows, mothers walking their children in parks, shoe salesmen, dentists, plumbers, etc., who have run into my mother and who absolutely love her. A certain cashier at a certain Daitch Shopwell begins to feel comforted and cheered when she sees my mother lumber through the IN door with her folded shopping cart.

At Christmas, my mother receives an inordinate number of packages and cards from near and far. Long letters arrive that begin, "My dear, dear friend," in tiny script. Someone is always remembering her many kindnesses, her smile, her help, her cheery good will. And what do I remember? I remember her telling me many times that she should never have had children, because children (meaning me since I was the only children she had left to get her notions from) only cause their parents pain and trouble. She told me not to set my sights too high because things never turned out as well as we wish them to. Why was she so pessimistic?

She said to me on the telephone today that she's been dreaming of me lately and it prompted her to call. Was everything all right? It was. Children fine. D. fine. House fine. Me fine. A little anemic, but fine. Yes, I'd been to the doctor. Was taking iron pills. Andrew was fine. Tall for his age, smart for his age. Nicholas was fine. The happiest of us all. Amanda was fine. Strong-willed, a replica of Andrew. And how was she? Oh, fine, fine. Living in Massachusetts for a while with a dear friend who was recuperating from an operation.

We none of us want to end up like our mothers. The mother in the park who only has to come on Fridays and holidays and who hates to return home so quickly after carpooling and who can't read novels because her time is too broken up and it takes too long, has a lot to say about her mother. She says:

"It's funny"—funny choice of words because it's far from funny—"I can see in many ways how I could be like my mother—not as far as being a fanatic cleaner—which she is—but in other ways. In my parents' marriage, my mother is the boss without question. My father is extremely intelligent. Extremely. He is probably one of the brightest people I have ever met, but you wouldn't know it just meeting him. My mother, without meaning to . . . it's a case where two people tore each other apart emotionally . . . they love each other but there has been this constant tearing. Both of them just a shambles emotionally. But always, she was the boss. The one we listened to. If we asked our father something and he answered differently from what her answer would have been, we would be punished. In our eyes, this negated him. Now I've gone the other way; I make a deliberate effort to build my husband up to the kids. I could manipulate them and point out that their father isn't there much. I could say, 'look at him, he's out working. Look at him, he's a jerk. He doesn't care about us at all.' But I don't. I don't want to be like my mother so I say, 'Our Daddy is special. Look how much our Daddy loves us.' "

The blonde activist has told us at least twice how sad she felt as a young girl watching her mother raising four children. "Oh, God. I'll have to do that," she thought and felt sad.

"Why sad?" we asked in a chorus.

"Because I saw what having those children did to her body. Her body was destroyed and then I'd watch her year after year bending down to child level, calluses on her heels, all out of proportion. I didn't want that to happen to me but I thought it had to."

Ann Sheridan's look-alike has very little to say about her mother but what she does say is succinct. "There are just the two of us," she says, "my sister and I. Normally, I would not like someone who has the personality traits of my sister. She's selfish, vain, shallow. But my sister and I get along very well. No sibling rivalry. No hidden hostility. And it's quite simple. We're united by a common enemy. My mother."

There's no proof that the possibility of evil I attribute to my mother could be true. She's never done anything evil to me, at least not the kind of evil I envision. She may have slapped me once or twice for a suspected looseness with men, which was unfounded. I wasn't loose. I was tight.

She has scrubbed my back, soothed me with all the ointments she keeps at hand when anything hurt me. She has ointments everywhere. Under the bed, over the bed—in the bed, for all I know. She's ever ready to whip them out and anoint my troubles away. She makes the bed in strange ways with strange sheets but it's comfortable. It smells like her, a special smell that's not altogether human . . . musty, pseudo-medicinal. A potion smell, ha, ha. My mother, the good witch. We have to get over the notion that witches are bad. If we have witches, there must be a need for witches, nature being so economical, etc., etc.

●

Perhaps they will be the symbols. Yes, he and the children will be ephemeral. Theirs will be the life I tuck away when the going gets rough or the busy holiday season rolls around. I was never too crazy for this world anyway. Too imperfect. Too many bad complexions to make people shy and hate themselves. Too many eyes set too close together. Too many big noses with large pores. Too many unanswered telephone calls, crippled egos, crippled legs, withered arms, withered loves. Too many sudden deaths, sudden bends in the road. Too many bombs bursting in air for my taste.

It's much better inside. "I'm going inside," she said haughtily, casting a disillusioned eye on the proceedings. In there, I'm my own person with none of the side effects. It's not lonely. The rent is never too high. The view is always perfect. No dues to pay. No guilt to pay.

•

I did fool Andrew. We're not having Boston scrod for dinner. We're having *Suprêmes de Volaille à l'Estragon.* The children are helping to pound the chicken breasts, snorting noisily in the grip of concentration. Their mouths hang loose and saliva drips unnoticed all over their chests.

"When Daddy comes home and asks who cooked this delicious dinner, I'll say you did, Nick. Nick helped to cook the chicken breasts. And Dad will say, 'Oh, I don't believe it.' "

"I'll punch him in the stomach," says Nick. He doesn't like the part about not believing. He takes it personally. When Andrew was his age, he delighted in our not-believing games. He'd comb his hair and come in for inspection. We pretended not to recognize him.

"Yes." I would turn around and look at him blankly. "Can I help you?"

"Mom, it's me. Your boy."

"That can't be. You're very neat and, while our boy is nice, he never looks that neat. Are you lost?"

"Well, uh . . . did your boy have two teeth missing because he fell down the stairs and swallowed them?"

"Why yes. How did you know?"

"Because the boy is me. Look! It's got to be me. See, my teeth are missing." I check him out and get an interested look on my face.

"Andy, is that you?" A gleam of recognition, finally a hug and kiss and a call to his father, "Look, it's Andy. I can hardly believe it, can you?"

We went through the scene over and over until we were sick to death of it. But not him. Children don't tire of repetition; they thrive on it. But Nicholas, he doesn't go for this delayed reaction stuff. He wants his approval right out. Heap it on. He devours the clumsiest praise.

My attention is not totally on the *Suprêmes de Volaille*, which the children have now mushed up into a beige-pink pyramid. The call from my mother needs tidying up. She left me in possession of her telephone number, a new unlisted number presumably meant to outfox a suspicious caller who either said nothing or said too much.

From time to time, I will have to dial these digits and relate to the voice on the other end. A voice that will be sullen if it has received the "canine" special, or garrulous and oily if it has received the preferred "human" special.

It's been a relief not seeing or talking to her this past year, although I knew it couldn't last. Now that she has surfaced, I realize there was some anxiety over her reappearance.

The anxiety over her reappearance began during the next-to-last meeting with the mystic. It was a Wednesday and the title on the program read, "Falsehood is Prophetic." I surmised that the mystic meant one of three things:

That lies came true.

That lies we presumed were original and spontaneous were really unsought prognostications.

That the title meant nothing and was the whim of a bored mystic wishing desperately to cover higher ground.

If he was a true mystic, seeing plainly what we merely suspected—our great and glorious possibilities—then he must have been bored with us, our supplicating eyes, our open mouths, our dumb and vacant stares.

We were a few minutes into our preliminary meditation and the mystic was quoting from Blake: "There is a moment in each day that Satan cannot find, nor can his watch fiends find it; but the industrious find this moment and it multiply, and when it once is found it renovates every moment of the day if rightly placed."

I found myself going down quickly into meditation, as if my innards were lying in wait for me. Without warning, I was murderously angry and began to vent blows, plunge daggers, empty the contents of numerous well-oiled guns on a slightly plump, defiant target. Artillery fire, a firing squad. I knew the creature. Her expressions sometimes stare back at me in the mirror and I've been known to tug at my chin when I'm nervous in the same way she does. She who has been the recipient of so many murderous thoughts was now receiving the actual, physically taxing murderous actions. How many ways could I kill her? It was a well-drilled plan and came off letter perfect. I had done in dear old Mom.

There was no blood, nor did she change position. She remained erect, arms outstretched, a sly smile on her thin lips. Anyone else would have bent under such blows, buckled under the vicious dagger attacks.

As suddenly as it began, the assault was over, leaving me satisfied with my day's work and tremendously interested. No sooner did I come up than I was ready to go down again and summon her up. She appeared easily into view, unimpaired. Like the coyote in the children's Roadrunner cartoons, she was back together as before. While still not crazy about her, I was content to let her be . . . at some distance from myself.

I recall something the mystic said—or is he saying it now *or* did I think of it myself. It doesn't matter. There can't be anything in mind, in life, that's greater than my ability to rout it out and keep it out of my affairs. If there were, life would be shit and it isn't.

As I recall this now in my custom-built designer kitchen, lightness fills my body. After such gross exertion, I'm suddenly a kite about to flutter off the ground. D. and I are dancing professionally, Ginger Rogers and Fred Astaire, now clasping hands, arms outstretched, now back to back, shoulders touching. We turn gracefully without letting go, parting and turning like a perfect zipper, stretching easily like newly applied rubber cement. We face each other, joined at the forehead, while our bodies stretch out behind us and begin to rise. We are floating in a world without words, without deductive reasoning. For a moment, free.

That's it. A small weighty secret is out, allowing me new lightness. Matricide, satisfying as it is, carries a stiff price tag. I've lost my innocence. D. and the children are guileless and I am knowing. With them, what you sees is what you gets. With me, what you see is what I have carefully allowed you to see. It never occurred to me that I did nothing with the knowingness; I could have done a lot but it just made me self-conscious. When did it happen? Maybe five, six years ago. Maybe forever. No, not forever. Even a few years back I was operating from a different point of view, without this burden. I was still having girlhood fantasies, dreaming of past lovers. For a long moment, I am wildly nostalgic for the girl I was. A particularly golden June afternoon comes vividly to mind.

Libby and I are in her garden, stooping down, thinning out the Swiss chard, both half-crazy with excitement over the sprouts that have pushed through. I snip off some tender shoots and stuff them in my mouth while she eyes me with mixed feelings. "You really should be putting these in the salad without cooking," I say. "They're delicious now. They'll only get tough and bitter later." She tastes the light green leaves I hand her and her face lights up. We were so happy to be where we were.

"Did you work before you married?" I asked.

"Huh," she rocks back on her heels and then decides to squat down all the way. "I worked and made quite a sum. What do you think? That all I know is this crap?" We giggled and snorted and fell over, spoiling some of the plants behind us.

She had a high-powered biggie in love with her and he did her dirt. I had a famous writer in love with me and he did me dirt. Did she flirt now? Was there a secret lover? Did she still have a yen for the high-powered biggie, and would she sleep with him if circumstances allowed? Giggle, giggle. Yes. Maybe. Who knows.

Our children play in the sun, looking like angelic figures from the holy cards of my Catholic childhood, while their mothers turn back the clock. Later, they sit dazzled because we know all the words to "Chattanooga Choo Choo."

I can go back to a younger, more innocent me, but that reminds me that someone else has seen me young lately. At the last meeting with the mystic, the man who always spoke to me put a girl in a hypnotic trance and asked her to scan my body. She sat directly in front of me, laughing now and then (in her trance) at some absurdity she saw. "I see her little," she said. "I see her as a little girl. She was cute. And happy. Smiling." Then she said, "Part of her lung is missing and there's a sort of outline of the missing part like a piece of clear plastic."

The man urged her to look further and she didn't say anything for a long time. I thought she'd gone to sleep and was feeling embarrassed. "I don't understand," she said finally. "Everything's in good order. Little spots here and there. An old kidney infection. Nothing serious though, she's healthy. But what I sense . . . what I see is a waiting. Everything waiting for a go-ahead."

"Thank you, Clara," said the man, and he brought her gently out of her trance. When she was fully alert, he said, "That was *my* lung you saw, Clara." He was reproachful, dissatisfied that she had seen me healthy. He didn't want to let me off so easily. He took a far-away seat and ignored me.

For myself, I was pleased that she had seen me as a happy child. I think, too, I know what Clara saw. I have been waiting. Waiting for them to grow up. To feed themselves. Dress themselves. Tie their shoes. To speak. To show their exceptional qualities. Waiting in tight adult situations. In hallways while something was going on inside. In vestibules. On stairs. In anterooms. On strange sidewalks. Trying to coax the children (perhaps even D.) into being quiet, still, polite, thoughtful, nonexistent. We wait together for Daddy to come home. For bedtime, naptime, Christmas. Summer. Death. We're future freaks, waiting endlessly for some promised emotional kick, our ship. I can't believe this is all there is for me.

Chapter Eleven

6:14 P.M. BY THE BEDROOM DIGITAL CLOCK. Kafkaesque, it appears to be riffling precisely through every minute of eternity.

Here is D., home now, neat as a pin. Pale blue Levi's, crinkle cotton shirt, mustachioed, hair modishly long and fluffy. At my urging, he has abandoned neckties, dress shirts, suits, vests, overcoats, links to the past. A simplified life will serve him well through any eventuality I may visit on him, good or bad. I'm preparing him as a good Mommy prepares her child for a visit to the dentist.

I usually can be found in the kitchen (where he is heading), but today I'm in the bedroom busily trying on dinner party clothes. The pile on the bed is getting higher and higher; nothing fits to my satisfaction.

I didn't want to be doing this when D. came home, because my attire is too provocative. He will take it as meaning something else, or it will remind him of what I don't want him to be reminded of. The silky black T-shirt fits snugly around my unrestrained breasts, precisely outlining my nipples, which look very precise. My breasts have always pleased me and I like the feel of the slinky fabric against my skin. Perhaps my wish not to be caught in provocative attire is simply an amateurish smoke screen for the real enchilada, which is (surprise, surprise) I *do* want to be caught in provocative attire. D.'s response is as expected. "What's that?" He puts down his parcels—*The New York Times*, a royal blue notebook holding his investment letters—without taking his eyes off my T-shirt. "That looks great . . . wow . . . I like it."

It isn't only the shirt; there's an air of sexuality permeating the room. A sense of indolence that's quite unusual for predinner spirits, which are usually verging on hostility, stomachs rumbling.

The sexuality could be coming from me, breaking loose. My customary predinner goblet of Gallo Chablis has warmed me more than usual. Three cheers for the Gallo Brothers. I feel an itch of sorts with no particular place to scratch. If it wasn't just us blindly judging ourselves, there would be obvious clues.

Amanda is languishing on our king-size bed, one hand in her mouth, the other tugging idly at the slim little crotch of her training pants. I cannot ignore her little plump hand. It sets me thinking about what she's doing and how it feels. The children's unconcern is startling. They can be eating with one hand and have the other below decks. And it's always unhurried.

So there you are, a strange turn of events. The old body gets you just when you least expect it.

When Andrew was in the hospital for a strange swollen gland, there was a woman in the waiting room whose child was seriously ill. It wasn't long after I arrived that she came over and whispered to me, "The sicker our little boy gets, the more my husband and I fuck." I kept my eyes glued to the *Ladies' Home Journal* on my lap. "We went away with another couple for a weekend of fucking. My mother sent us to the mountains for a change of scene. 'A change will do you both good,' she said. The only change was who we fucked. We switched partners. My little boy is very ill," she said, as if to excuse herself. I see the very same woman occasionally at the supermarket and she dawdles at the pickles, condiments and spices aisle to avoid me.

"Your body is your friend," my old maid gym teacher used to tell us in college. "Listen to it and heed what it says. It will never lead you astray."

I am very concerned about my body. I'm starting to recognize the pull of gravity and these days, when I'm tired, I feel it first in my nether regions—my uterus—the pelvic floor, they call it. "Sweeties," the gym teacher would tell us, "you have to make believe there's a quarter in your backside and hold it without letting go. Do this every time you're waiting for a green light and you'll survive childbirth in style." She made us get down on all fours to get our inner parts aligned. Weekly, she reminded us that only chance and good thoughts kept our tubes, ovaries, uteri, from shifting around willy-nilly. There was nothing solid to keep them in place. She was right and it saddens me (not in a vain way but in an emotional sense) that my body is feeling the pull of time. It saddens me even more that, to date, I have had no adequate way of expressing all of this to my lover nor even a strong impulse to try. No sense of immediacy.

D. comes home too late to salvage anything here. By six-thirty we're doped up. Too much of each other, too much of our gorgeous four walls, too much silence, yelling, television. The children usually rush at him with frantic screeches and I either mumble hello or simply look up dumbly. Today, however, I'm alert. Desire does that for you. When you feel like making love nothing else can distract you. The Stills, the Riddleys, D. and I. Everything falls by the wayside. Every little move counts and I don't want to miss a thing.

I kiss him full on the mouth which surprises him. If I could have it all my way, he wouldn't say anything. He would not look surprised or say, "Umm, that's nice." I would like it if both of us could proceed without saying or doing anything other than what we would ordinarily say and do.

"Umm, that's nice," says D. and searches for another, longer kiss.

169

"We're having a good dinner," I say quickly, determined to call the shots as long as possible.

D. proceeds to exchange his work clothes for his breakfast clothes, switching shirts at the last minute. Andrew comes in, having wrenched himself from *Star Trek* to greet his father. He approaches with a loving and surprised look. "Dad, I like that shirt." He puts his arms around D.'s neck, forcing him to stoop over and allow himself to be kissed and caressed. D. grimaces. He doesn't enjoy this kind of fondling by his seven-year-old son, and, when Andrew leaves him and idly switches on the television in our room, the pained look remains on his face.

"I don't know how to react when he strokes and kisses me like that," he whispers to me. "I don't like it. There's something about it that makes my skin crawl." It occurs to me that skins are crawling all over this house. Here we are smack in the middle of the Touching Decade, marathon weekend touching retreats being initiated all over the country and nobody here wants to be touched. "It must be the way a woman feels when some guy is doing things she doesn't like." He looks at me out of the corner of his eye. He wants to beat me to some expected put-down. "Here it comes. She's going to zing me now, folks. You're going to say that's how you feel when I touch you." He's officially joking but there's enough truth in the remark to jolt me.

"When we were first married you used to do things I did find creepy. All the ear business."

"Most women like that. How was I supposed to know?"

"Most women! Most women!" I can't believe how angry this makes me. "How do you know what most women want? Even if you . . . let's be generous and say you've copulated with two hundred women in your day and suppose they all had the most erogenous ears extant. That would still not give you the right to say, in that self-righteous voice, most women like this or most women like that."

"All right. All right." His voice and face have the tone and look of, "Oh, boy. Here comes the heightened-consciousness bit."

I feel awkward saying these feminist things. I'm not hitting the real issues. If Betty Friedan were to come aboard here and take inventory, there would be more insidious assaults going on and she would laugh or sneer over my puny issue. However, I'm encouraged by my steady and unemotional beginning. "Women . . . I myself always feel I'm not measuring up to some mythical sexual dynamo who loves it all day, all night. In the kitchen, the bathroom, wherever the mood hits her." Here are more feelings for Betty to sneer at. I feel guilty about my heightened consciousness. I feel his sense of impatience with me and I'm sympathetic to it. Some part of me, if you can believe the criss-crossedness of it, is actually on his side against me. For so long I've felt responsible for everyone's mood and now I'm a genius at getting inside their heads and working out the feelings.

I voice none of this. Men have been deciding long enough when things get repetitive and boring. "Don't give me that 'Oh, God, you're going to start on the liberation business' look. If all this makes you uncomfortable, think how uncomfortable it has made me."

"Why didn't you tell me about it? You never tell me anything."

The children are now totally engrossed in Mr. Spock and his adventures, and D. motions to me to follow him out of the bedroom. We return to the chaos of the kitchen and D. sits down at his usual place. The bread crumbs from the chicken breasts are scattered over the floor and I pick up a broom and begin to sweep them up (hiding behind my broom?). An old black waiter that I knew as a young woman once warned me about sweeping under chairs. It came to no good for young girls, he said. If you swept under the chair of a young woman, she was doomed never to marry. Was I double-daring the

Fates by sweeping under D.'s chair? Would I now lose my hubby? It's strange what comes to you when you're all charged up.

D. begins. "You throw me crumbs of yourself and your feelings and want me to be happy with the crumbs and not begrudge you the whole slice of bread. You've never opened up to me and you're not really opening up to me now. In fact, you never tell me anything. You never speak in bed or when we're embracing. Silent Susie. It's maddening. Then, when you want to let slip some trivial inner thought . . . perhaps to you it feels important but the words are ordinary. Very ordinary. It doesn't sound important and although I'm not aware of turning away or humiliating you, perhaps somewhere deep inside I'm really saying, 'screw you.' I don't want your stingy bits of self-revelation. I'd rather have nothing and I'd like to show you as well that I don't need them."

He's right. I can't speak. Victoriana has me by the vocal cords. And also, I suppose, Sister Francisca. Sister Francisca is lurking in the dark as she used to at boarding school, ready to pounce when everyone was settled down and relaxed in their beds. Ready to yank off covers and direct her vicious flashlight in the general direction of our genitals looking for subversive activity. What's going on here? Are nightgowns in place? If everything is in order, the blankets are replaced, the searching light turned on the floor. If hands are between legs for warmth or comfort, they are yanked out by the elbow without explanation. "Hands on top of covers, girls," she would say sternly and swish off making her beads knock against each other.

So now, of course, I say absolutely nothing in bed. And besides, did Ginger Rogers talk to Fred Astaire? June Haver to Fred MacMurray? Jackie to Jack? My mother to my father?

"I can understand that," I say, flipping the lever that relaxes all my muscles. He has rescued me from the absurd. I'm not going crazy. But then I remember that solving our communication problem is not what I'm after. That still would not take me where I want to go. It would simply keep me where I am, more embroiled than ever. In a togetherness that has ceased to appeal to me.

And if I did speak, what would I tell him? To kiss me here and not there. To put it in gently or shove it in harshly. To coax me or demand it. Should I spend my spare time thinking of precisely how I want it? How I want to be touched and handled? Or perhaps I should do the handling, call the shots. What are red hot lovers doing up and down the street? Playing postman or doctor? Or is nobody doing it to anybody in all those *trompe-l'oeil* bedrooms?

If I could have it all my way, I would make love in a pitch-black bedroom without a word being said. I don't see anything wrong with that, although I suspect others might, including D., so I keep my preferences to myself. My objective is to keep D. from straying from my script as much as possible. Lately, I can tolerate the television. If it were a talk show, I'd like to listen to what was being said up to the last minute.

Star Trek is over, the children are straggling in, expecting to be fed. We *are* having a good dinner but, when we're finally settled with each of our plates sporting a chicken breast, rice with pine nuts, mixed green salad, the children begin to decide what they can and cannot tolerate on their plates. The mushrooms are picked out of the salad, the nuts out of the rice. Neat piles of food begin to decorate the outer rims of their plates. The chicken is divided into two piles—the portion they do and don't have to eat in order to be allowed dessert. Nine-tenths of our dinner table conversation revolves around what they feel about the food they are eating.

When I make my earthy lentil stew with neck bones and plump grains of barley and cracked wheat, Andrew tells me it's like eating a horse's mane. He will choose an early bedtime and an empty stomach rather than eat it or taste it or smell it or look at it, which leaves me contemplating what a horse's mane would taste like for the remainder of the evening.

After a few meaningless bites, he decides this dinner is intolerable as well and asks if he may have dessert.

"No."

"Can I just not have dessert or do I have to go to bed?"

"You have to go to bed."

"OK, I'll go to bed."

"You don't have to go to bed."

"But I can't have dessert, right?"

"Right."

"OK, but can I just have a sip of your wine?"

"Yes." He takes a sip.

"It's like getting a hundred flu shots on your tongue all at once."

He has learned most of the rules for human interaction. When to charm, when to move fast, when to resist, when to feign giving in. The only thing he hasn't learned is when to stop. Where else could I get such pure life experience?

Nick has stored his entire dinner in his cheeks and has managed to eat and enjoy two portions of dessert without swallowing one gram of his dinner. It's revolting and makes me angry, but there's nothing I can do about it. That's the thing about children, they can always get you in the end.

The only one whom I can trust sporadically not to "get me" is D., who looks very appealing in his workman's blue shirt. Desire makes me generous and forgetful. Where could I get a better friend than this? Who could better share my sense of irony? Hadn't he walked behind me through each laborious ascent up the hospital elevator to the maternity ward while some officious nurse held me prisoner in a backless wheelchair while my pregnant back begged for support? When I ask if I can walk and they say no, doesn't he always say, "No, of course not. She might be comfortable"? Is he perhaps the perfect husband? The ultimate Mr. Right?

He looks so strong and vibrant reading the label of the

Pepperidge Farm Lemon Crunch Cookies. "Lemon comes after table salt."

"What?"

"In the list of ingredients, lemon comes after the table salt."

"Jesus, why call it lemon? I always trusted Pepperidge Farm."

"Because of that wheezy old guy who does the commercials?"

"No. Not because of that . . . well, I guess, yes because of that. The image I had of them is a good one, but they shouldn't call them Lemon Crunch cookies."

"You're so naive," he says and rises to put his dishes in the sink.

He's wrong. I'm not naive, I'm more knowing than even I suspect. Now, for instance, after a day fraught with misgivings, half-plans, murky resolutions, I'm ready to toss all that momentum away for a roll in the hay. And here's where the knowingness comes in. I know that a night of lovemaking will clear the air, and all the questions he has been asking so insistently will be put aside for a while, giving me the time I need to perfect my plans. I don't yet know just what those plans are, but I'm sure they will be very clear to me if I persist. I'm meditating now for the proper outcome.

D. is fed, satisfied, ready to stretch out on his Eames chair and enjoy the fruits of his labors. It's dark outside and I know my chatter will not have to compete with birds, strange aircraft, a strange weather pattern, a cold front passing through or settling in. A screech owl might whimper in the night but he wouldn't be able to see anything.

"D.," I begin in a soft voice I know will get his attention. He has reached for his *HOLT Investment Advisory*. "I have decided something." The royal blue investment notebook is put out of reach of tempted hands, eager eyes. D. visibly prompts himself to sit and listen. "I'm going to give a series of dinner parties to repay everyone we owe a dinner. I'm going to put the couples together imaginatively. That'll be a challenge, don't you think, to put strange mixtures together and see how it works. I'll make something that can be prepared ahead of time so I can enjoy my own party. Tara can come and play with the children. I'll arrange it all tomorrow. We'll have one each week and that will take us into summer when all the beach socializing begins. But D., there's only one thing and I know it's silly . . . well, I know it sounds silly but I don't have anything to wear, nothing I feel right about."

"Wear that black thing. In fact, why not put that black thing on right now?"

I pick up *The New York Times* to hide my disappointment. I would have been perfectly willing to casually follow him into the bedroom and on some innocent pretext or other begin naturally to make love. But now, those leering eyes and the suggestion that I slip into some black, slinky thing, braless, has set me back a bit. Why can't he just shut up.

I know it's my fault. He has been ready to *communicate* for a few years now. He would like to talk out our lovemaking until each knew what to do for the other. I hate to talk things out. Sometimes I think of something to discuss and . . . yes . . . I'd like to have a conversation about something other than what we're doing. But ardor means different things to different people and men like to concentrate. They take anything that is not completely serious and on the subject as a sign of what . . . boredom? Lack of interest? Incomplete desire? Humor is out. I wish it were in.

The *Times* hides my face but secretly I'm watching him. I see signs that he's aging now. Small signs that come and go with the quality of his night's sleep, the ease of his work, the lightness of his heart. As he reads his investment advice by a small direct lamp, the light throws shadows on his face that play with his age. Now he's younger. Now he's older and when I see him older a wave of wedding day blues hits me right in the labanza. My God, he'll be old and I didn't keep my part of the bargain. What good will all this thinking do me when I'm holding his hand on his deathbed or at the lawyer's office, or in court? Somehow, I feel, no matter what we do, I will always hold his hand. After all, I'm not immune to basic human feelings.

There are times when I love him beyond reason or I'm grateful to him beyond reason, whichever comes first. Will I end up like Nicholas, my middle child, falling in love after the fact? Forever mourning yesterday, rubbing my hands and smacking my lips over a feast of guilt and regrets like a mental necrophiliac in a field of open graves? It boggles the mind.

Sometimes, when we're sitting like this, alone at night, strange noises, creakings and thin whistles surprise us.

"That's the house cooling off," he will say. I would never in a million years associate the creaking noises of the night with the fact that the house was cooling off—that wood and steel and plaster were changing shape with the temperature.

One of his wise/peculiar friends told me very early in our marriage, "It's the differences that keep you together. Don't ever try to make him exactly like yourself." I hate tricky sayings and I didn't like that one until recently, when I started getting interested in who I was myself.

He is not a hail fellow well met. A glad hand. He could not become a regular at the Rotary Club or the Lions Club. He couldn't sell the Brooklyn Bridge, as the expression goes, unless the buyer were a sensitive soul who believed that less is more and took D.'s unflashy presentation as appropriate. D. is completely lacking in pretense, which is ironic, since I am forever pretending. Pretending to be this, pretending to be that. Not to fool anyone, God knows, but simply to exist. It's an efficient way for me to exist. There is a movie ad in which an unshaven Jack Nicholson is telling an intensely interested Maria Schneider, "I used to be somebody else . . . but I traded myself in." Why is this news? A line like that has absolutely no poignancy for a jolly suburban matron. I just turn to my spice shelves bordered with colorful Portuguese tiles, select a jar of home-grown ginger for my meat loaf *en croûte* and think, "Why are you saying this, you silly man? Why are you so interested, you silly woman?"

Fortunately for me, as he has reminded me many times, he is a sexually vigorous man. Sensual in every way. His memories are sensual. He remembers his first day of kindergarten and tells it to the children often when they have to begin something new and he wants to prepare them. We all know it by heart. Mrs. Howland played a Sousa march on the piano and all the children marched around the room, their little feet going clap, clap on the wooden floor. I can just see D.'s five senses taking it all in . . . Mrs. Howland's purple dress, the low January sun streaming in through twenty-foot-high windows, his mother waiting when it was over in the crisp winter air.

All the assaults he remembers from childhood were assaults to his senses. "My father not only bought used cars," he will recall, "but used tires. We'd go to the used tire store and he'd take me with him. I was impatient to get out of there but he'd just whistle in that rambling way he had. He'd whistle and look. You can imagine how long it took to decide on buying used tires. In 1936 we had a 1932 car, a Plymouth. In 1943 we had a 1938 car. Sometimes he had his tires regrooved and recapped and once he bought recapped ones. That's what it was like in the Depression. They're all right, I guess." He rolls it over in his head. "They put recapped tires on trucks."

Unlike his own parent, he doesn't put his children through long anxious waits. He is a man who inspires confidence.

In the afternoon, I think about how he will comfort me. Why do I think in the evening I need comforting? He makes me feel properly married and I remember well the day that thought sunk in. The day I knew I was no longer a separate entity but rather part of two, an inherent combination of events. One end of a rope in tension. One end of a two-way conversation. The receptacle of half a thought to be finished by someone else. Half a punchline. A divisible number.

That day came when he approached us one evening in early summer after his day's work. We were sitting on the lawn—it was just Andrew and I then—and he approached us in an almost staged way and held out a parcel to me.

"I bought you a lady's hammer," he said.

He had watched me over the weeks putting together our new cottage. Half-screwing screws, half-bolting bolts in my lady way. Everything held. It seemed tight. I didn't see any reason to turn the screws any further. He didn't demand this work of me, I chose to do it, and now he was protecting me, in a sense, from the realities of a man's world. He bought me a lady's hammer so I could do my lady's number. Son of a gun. (It was as delicate as a hammer could be and still make sense.)

The idea that someone else was sorting out my life, coming to conclusions, making small, beneficial decisions for my welfare was overwhelmingly comforting to me then, touchy as I was after childbirth.

It's amazing how much we've learned to say to each other without uttering a single word. But the trouble with that kind of language is there's too much latitude. Take one wrong turn in that kind of conversation and you will arrive at the wrong place from then on. That's not hatred you read in my eyes. It's fear. Fear because I've gained five pounds and I don't know what lies ahead for me.

Women are mysterious, you know. Labyrinthian. They have cycles like the moon. They're cosmic. Always doing furtive, private things and it all takes place inside them.

He recalls the stilted conversations of his youth about the vagaries of women. "We'd drive two hundred miles in an old car to the lake and then my sister couldn't go in the water. All they could tell me was, 'Son, for a few days each month, your mother and sister can't go in the water.' Why not? It drove me crazy. I wanted to know. We have snapshots of my sister lying in the sun with her bathing suit on and I remember asking her, 'Why don't you go in the water, for God's sake? It's hot!' She wouldn't answer. Just looked away and ignored me."

I am mystified by him as well, by his raw, simple and frightening emotions. Even though throughout the year we both agree that it's infantile and sheeplike to buck crowds just to give each other a present on December 25th, or birthdays or anniversaries, when we can just as well do it any other day with calmness and unrushed certainty, he will surprise me on the right day with the right present. He covers me at night. He has a picture of me stuck in his drawer at work and loves to be surprised by it when he happens to open that particular drawer, instead of having me stuck on his desk with the kids like a sentinel or to show us off like trophies.

I'm still surprised by how handsome he is and I'm still glad to point him out as my husband at strange parties and when he meets the kids' teachers and when he meets the man at the deli who has known me with uncombed hair and crying children.

If our dreams were better I could begin to have some faith in all this. I want to see snatches of happiness in our dreams. Small things. Arriving at our destinations. Waking to a surprising calm instead of the clammy fears. No longer the dark lady of literature, I want to see green rolling hills and jump with ease over hurdles and land, unhurt, smiling on the other side. It will give us a secret with which to face the world.

I want to stop depending on ringing telephones and cheerful mailmen and rattle away the hours in a new clear-headedness. No longer little baby face. Babyface Nelson, that was me, I'll say. On the one hand, cute, demure. On the other, knocking my dear ones out all over the place. Now, what the hell, I'm simply not afraid and there is a marvelous appeal. It's better than big boobs or high cheekbones or a clear and unlined mouth. It will be sure ground I cover and I won't have to tread that road again.

Chapter Twelve

11:03 THE LAST TIME I LOOKED at the numbers glowing in the dark.

I am lying very still in my bed trying to recall the orgasm I experienced not fifteen minutes ago in minute detail. Ignoring the itch of my thigh, the hunger pangs in my stomach, I am trying to reconstruct the pleasure trip. What was it now? A fully extended telescope, each rung a pleasure transmitter, carrying this urgent rolling ball to my head where a potent but unfrightening implosion takes place. Secret folds and linings of my brain and body are suddenly tumescent, bulging with potential. I'm fully extended, everything outstanding, and something's going to give. I can feel the inside of my body, so long unvisitable, now giving way, the perfect place to be. Vaginal versus clitoral? Mine is cerebral.

I think of how it was in the early days, when any place was a challenge. We did it on the pine needles of a pine forest, in the middle of Great South Bay, in his Porsche on the Connecticut Turnpike at ninety miles an hour.

Now, at the very least, I have this terrific sex machine at my command. Why give it up? I suddenly see and feel myself so grotesquely powerful, physically huge, looming. It won't last. The power will ebb and flow.

Life stretches before me a long series of intimate satisfactions, a variety of orgasms, each one different. The infinite variety D. claims for the beach scene, for his beloved horizons, sunsets and weather patterns, I will claim for my orgasms. I will say, "D., I want a different orgasm every day." If it's to be a treadmill, let it be a treadmill riddled with orgasms.

D. is snoring softly beside me. A perfect genteel snore, but I'm too worked up to sleep. He waited a decent interval before conking out. I talked about the children to short circuit any other subject. I said I was worried about Nick. He was whining too much and full of worries. Worries about disaster.

"They worry about you and each other," I said. "When that man sideswiped you on the road the other day, I think it was wrong to let them see the car all smashed up. Every time we pass that spot on the road, Nick asks me about it. He wants to be sure you were in the right. I was impatient with him today. I told him not to ask about it anymore. But he cares more about asking than he cares about my anger because he brought it up again on our way home, which means he's really worried about you."

"Worried about what?"

"He wants to know what it would take to kill you. Or maybe he's worried that you didn't get killed because we're always telling him that when you get hit by a car, you get killed. Now he wonders if we're lying to him or if you're really dead and this is how it is to be dead . . . no change at all."

"I think Nick does care more than the others. He puts his little arm around my neck at night when I lie next to him to say goodnight. When I feel that skinny little arm around my neck . . . I don't know. Sometimes I think I love him . . . I couldn't love him any more if he were an only child."

"But why is he so insecure?"

"It's a phase. They're all so bright. Today he said he realized something. He used the word 'realize.' How can a little kid like that realize anything?"

•

I feel like prowling the empty house. The night prowler. As I leave the bedroom, closing the heavy door carefully behind me, I hear noises on the steps. It's Andrew with the first of his bad dreams. He's still asleep and groping up the stairs. Running from something? To something?

I sit him next to me on the stairs and shake him gently. "Andy, Andy. It's Mom. Are you having a bad dream?"

He looks at me confused. "Mom?"

"Yes. Are you having a bad dream?"

"I guess so."

"Cement gorillas?"

"No. Just regular ones."

"Angry ones?"

"No. Not too scary this time. Daddy told me to point at them. He said if I pointed at them, they'd get smaller."

"Yes?"

"I pointed and kept pointing."

"And . . . did they get smaller?"

"No. They stayed the same."

"But they weren't too scary?"

"Yeah."

"Well, that's almost the same. Come on, let's go back to bed."

"Mom?"

"Yes."

"Could you stay with me a little while until I go back to sleep?"

"OK."

I'm not aware of any particular close feeling as I lie there next to him. I hold his damp little hand in mine and wonder if my own good sense is beginning to pull us gently apart. After all, he's seven, the age of reason, and I've been a pusher long enough. There's an overstimulated pushing reflex at work here. My pushing muscles are distorted with exercise and nobody likes what I've become. They look at each other with knowing looks. (Not only my own dear kin but women do it to each other.) We roll our eyes and make a little shoving gesture with the heel of our hand and everyone knows that a big *pusher* has just passed by. I shovel the food in their mouths. Shovel the books down their brains. Shovel the right clothes, the galoshes, the mittens, the hats with ear flaps over their resisting wriggling bodies. It's not a pretty sight, but I'll repair my image later when they're gone and nobody calls.

I'll sit alone after other breakfasts pushing the toast crumbs into crazy little patterns and think quietly about myself. If we do a good job we won't see much of them later. If we don't, we'll see too much of them. That's my law of inverse action. Wash the car and it rains. Clean the living room and your husband will drag in firewood. Get too fussy over company dinner and the guests will quarrel and leave early.

I remember seeing a movie in which a robust teen-ager recounts to the psychologist during a family session how much he hated his parents for being old. His mother had had him at forty-three. "Who needed their old genes, their old crummy sperm and eggs? When they came to school, I was ashamed of their wrinkles and the way they shuffled along. I wanted them to die."

So no matter. You can't win as a parent. Either you care too much or not enough. Worry too much or not enough. Feed them too well or not at all. Build them up or tear them down. If you win, you've lost. So it's best not to expect to win. If you did, how could they wrench themselves away from you? Why would they want to?

I'm so afraid of their not turning out well. Nothing on earth—no editorial in *The New York Times*, no brainy article in *Psychology Today*—is going to convince me that I don't have everything to do with the way they turn out. It's more frightening to think it's out of my control. After all, what's a little chemical combination next to my determination? And what does turning out well mean? Turning out well for them? Or for me? Did I turn out well?

●

Once tucked in, Andrew drifts off quickly to sleep. I notice that the drawers of his dresser are gaping open, clothes spilling out. There are dirty socks everywhere and I make a mental note to come back in the morning and straighten things out.

I'll get a cleaning lady, I think, even if she isn't thorough and breaks everything. I'll start picturing my house clean and orderly and the right little cleaner will show up at my door. I have to make a list of all the things I want to imagine, but the most important ones first, working alternately from the outside in and from the inside out. Now I'm just working from the inside out but it's not going fast enough. But maybe it is and this very idea to clean up this place is just what's needed.

I might even go back to work. Amanda will be in nursery school in September. They'll all be gone for three full hours. I'm sure there are jobs for people like me. It couldn't just be any job, though. We don't need the money. It would have to be something that I loved and that gave me satisfaction. I'll go to one of the Mother's Morning Out talks they're always giving at the Methodist Church. They'll know where I should start. Or is it Meaningful Mornings Out? Or is it Mourningful Meanings Out? Ha, ha. There are ads in the *Pennysaver:* WOMEN bored or broke—earn extra bux, flex. hrs. kit supplied.

I could go back to my old job writing sexy, dumb ads for men's shirts, ads that said, "Hey, shirt. I hear you're permanently pressed. Wanna prove it?" Or sexy sexist things for women's wear: "Did you laugh too much, Amanda? Did you say the right things? All he'll remember is how great you looked in your Arnel raincoat."

What about all the things I've learned in the last ten years? They should count for something. I know how to make Duck *en gelée.* Eggs Ranchero surrounded by perfect rosettes of mashed potatoes, seven of the eight steps to an unforgettable buffet. I'm so finely tuned to the insouciance of fresh dill, I cut it at an angle to release an additional bitter tart juice to the dish. I can tie a scarf twenty-three ways. Stretch meat loaf for unexpected company. Hem pants quickly with iron-on tape. Make cheap tablecloths out of irregular sheets. Cut the children's hair. Make cosmetics from friendly old stand-bys on my pantry shelves.

I know how to ward off heart trouble through proper diet (or vice versa). Four surprising ways to decorate with pictures. That to bread a really super breast of chicken, which can then be the heart of twenty-three fabulous chicken dishes, the breast must be scrupulously dry (as dry as a Bedouin's instep, as Fred Allen would say).

I know that pulling the covers over your head in sleep reduces the oxygen you get by 20 percent and increases the carbon dioxide tenfold (could you then, if you stayed in bed too long, swaddle yourself to death?). That overweight women crave sex more than average-weight women. (Discovered in a study trying to prove the opposite, ha, ha.) I know the fun of making chocolates. How to tuft.

As for the dinner party circuit, I think I'll have to pass. At the last dinner party I gave (which may have set me up for my present misgivings) two of the guests, the McIntyres, found out so much about each other it was embarrassing. We were talking about husbands and wives taking separate planes and Mrs. McIntyre said it was a good idea in general but didn't matter too much in her case because she didn't know who in the world would take her children if she were to die. The husband glared at her and said, "Sylvia," in a long-drawn-out way; it was both a question and a reprimand.

"Well," she said meekly to the father of her children, "would you take them?" He began to sputter again and she demurred that of course she was kidding.

I was with her. I didn't think he would take them either and I know what drove her to say that. It confirms what I've always felt—women feel the children are really theirs and the men are just very nice to put up with it all.

If it is inevitable that I will follow in my mother's footsteps, perhaps I should get on with it. Perhaps, by hanging on, I'm becoming a Mr. Spock in a shipful of earth people. As Andrew says (taking his philosophical tidbits from *Star Trek*), a Vulcan can't stand pain, his mind goes crazy. He turns against everything. But he can hold pain for quite a while before it overtakes him. His sun is different from our sun. He can stand blinding light for a while. Not forever, but for a while. He's not immediately crippled by the misfortunes that cripple others. He can hang on a little longer.

Then, too, we can't rule out the possibility that there will be a very definite sign. I've always looked for signs. A sign here. A sign there. O Lord, O Life, give me a sign. If the line is busy, don't call back; it is a sign. Are the children all there is?

Are they as close as we come to the mystery of life and death and the differences and similarities in each? In the end, will I say, the children were everything? I have to see myself as the explorer, the patient private eye, the waiting stalker. Waiting out events to see what we shall see . . . *I went to the animal fair. The animals all were there. The big baboon by the light of the moon was combing his light brown hair.*

Ending up like my mother is not what's really frightening. What's really frightening is that the world as I know it, my round oak table, my cashmere sweaters, the 1971 Chateauneuf du Pape I'm so fond of, the Tiffany look-alike lamp that looks precisely the way I want it to look, the enormous Swedish ivy plant that I've nursed from three pathetic clippings, the stone fireplace—all these very substantial spatial things are as ephemeral as steam from a tea kettle, exhaust from his sports car, or my visible breath on a cold winter's day. If I take my attention away, they will cease to exist.

My world, as I know it, exists only in my consciousness, and the whole exercise in acquiring and furnishing and maintaining my present mode of life (including all emotional entanglements) is so much busy work. I've been dealing in bits and pieces of reality as if they were the whole thing. I've been embracing absurdities while the most engrossing possibilities lay dormant and ignored. The motives were not of my choosing and I didn't know I had chosen them. I've been paying attention to insipid particulars and ignoring the heart of the matter. Marriage, should we or shouldn't we? Children, should we or shouldn't we? Psychiatry. Breast-feeding. Television. Should we or shouldn't we? War. The Country. The city. Should we or shouldn't we? The Smiths. The Browns. The Greens. Women's Lib. Birth Control Pills. Love. Should we or shouldn't we? Private schools or public. Butter or Margarine. Sleep-away camp or togetherness? Europe or the Americas. The Parthenon or Yellowstone Park. Should I stay or should I go?

When we part, how will it be? Will the judge lean over and confront us with a slightly limp wrist and inquire smugly: "Well, what happened to you, my dears? Incompatibility?"

"Oh, no! We were compatible to a fault. Dipping into each other's plates. Invading each other's dreams, finishing each other's sentences. I knew which stories he would tell at parties by the way his eyebrows arched. He knew what I would say on the telephone by the way I tugged at the cord."

"Well, then what?" the judge would ask impatiently.

"We simply wanted to lead our lives, your honor. To live them out."

The way it is now, he knows I have a sinus headache from the tone of my voice. I know his stomach is acting up from his conversational pauses. I can see a time, not far off, when we will be mute and simply grimace our way through life. We will know to the letter how our lives are going. The particulars are just so much repetition, what we're really after is a reading on our happiness quotient.

How do you feel this morning? Did you have a good sleep? How was your day? Did you get the work you wanted? Are you glad to come home at night? Do you like the children? What about the baby's face? Do you think it's beautiful? Do you think she looks like me? Do you think I'm beautiful? Do I look my age? Younger? How much younger?

I changed the sheets today, does the bed feel good? How are your Eggs Ranchero? Too much pepper? Oh, I forgot you don't like pepper. Aren't the shrimp delicious? Are the kids getting to you? Which one do you think looks most like me? Which one do you love the most? Why do you keep making that noise? Yes, I hear it. You're letting the air out slowly through tight lips and it makes my skin crawl. Is something wrong? Why are you so quiet? Do you have something on your mind? Why are you upset? What are *you* so happy about? Did you have a good swim? Did you have a good time? Does your knee still hurt? Are you still having trouble with your eyes? Did you call your father? Do you like my hair this way? Would you rather I let it grow? Are you mad because I bought the cheap birdseed and the birds aren't eating it? Are you mad because I don't like birds? Are you mad because I made the spinach salad that doesn't agree with you? Are you mad because I read in bed last night and woke you up? Why don't you ever get mad? Why don't you ever scream the way I do?

Did you notice I didn't talk about myself at all at the party last night? Did you notice I changed the subject every time the opportunity to talk about the children came up? Did you notice I asked them what they were doing and how they felt and how their business was going and whether they had felt the ramifications of the gas shortage and the money shortage and the shortage of ethics in twentieth-century America?

Do you think I love you? Do you think I love the children? Which one do you think I've ruined the most? Are you mad because the laundry breaks all the buttons off your shirts and I won't iron them at home? Do you wish I were neater? Are you glad you married me? Are you glad we had the children? If you didn't know the children, would you think it was better to have children or not to have children? Do you think the last ten years of your life have been terrible, a little happy, very happy, or very terrible or none of the above? Do you think I'm too fat? Does my rear look too big in these pants? Would you rather I didn't wear them? Is this sweater too tight?

Why don't you leave me? Don't you feel like leaving me sometimes? Don't you think you could be happier with someone else? How can you love me after all the things I've done to you? What do you love most about me? Why do you always cover me at night? Did you know my father used to do that?

Why are you worried about your business? You're going to be rich just like my father. Don't you know I married someone just like my father? Are you mad because I said shit in front of the children? Do you care what the neighbors think? Do you want to be a pillar of the community? The salt of the earth? The rock of Gibraltar?

Do I irritate you? Are you happy? What was the happiest time of your life? Do you think anyone's happy? Have you ever known a happy person? Do you think we have a good marriage? Do you think we have a good sex life? Do you know anyone who has a good marriage? Do you know anyone who has a good sex life? Do you think Raquel Welch has a good sex life, or Henry Kissinger? Do you think a good sex life is a myth? Do you think a good marriage is a myth? Do you think people won't marry in another hundred years and they'll laugh at us just like we snicker at sultans and aghas who have a hundred wives or more? Do you know you have a high-pitched laugh when you're nervous?

Why do the kids always get hurt when I leave them with you? Why do they always lose their mittens? Why do you always run outside to look at an airplane when I'm trying to tell you something important?

Are we experiencing future shock? Does evolution have us by the balls?

I don't know why I'm always talking about leaving as if I'm really going to leave. What is it? A mutilated cell not doing a proper job in my medulla oblongata? The question keeps popping up like a boring jack-in-the-box and now—post-orgasmic, clear-headed—I see it for what it is—a diversionary tactic. Even so, it has wormed its way in, and that's all you need, one little wormy thought and the cells begin to multiply like an irresponsible amoeba.

Who am I kidding? Where would I go with my three little dependents and where would I place my hopes and dreams, not to mention my love, which is lying in wait, ready to pounce.

Like a crazy, pregnant salmon, I've been willing the swim upstream not because I really want to go but because I wanted to be . . . what? Effective? To write my own script? If I *am* a victim of evolution, so what? I can join the spiritually sly and see it all in a new light. Stop giving energy to the problem and fall in love with the solution. The mystic says once we fall in love with the solution all ideas necessary to its accomplishment will tumble down around us.

After all, they don't own me or my emotions. I can give them my attention, my good will, my tears once in a while when they marry or break a record, or break an arm. When they cause me pain and anguish, I can go in and correct the pain and anguish in myself. Rub it out. I can see them in a Hegelian light—a blending of opposites able to cope with whatever life dishes out without my degeneration to help them along.

They won't like what's happening and be suspicious. They'll cling to me like crazy marsupials and D. will, too, in a different way. The children will be the first to know when something really good is going on. What do they say? Children are emotional geniuses. If that's so, they will soon sense that something is going on in dear old Mom that's better than chenille bathrobes, Oxford shoes and apple pie. That this old Mom isn't going to be hanging on their futures, their presents, their successes or failures for dear life. She's going to be out. Or rather in.

As for D., our relationship is not an electronic impulse to be turned off like the war on television. We're real! I married him because he wore a hat to work and once, when we were dressing for a duty party, he brushed his shoes like mad and then turned to me and said, "This is going to be the kind of party where your shoes show a lot."

There was a time when we had skied all day in brilliant sunlight without goggles and I awoke the next morning with huge swollen slits where my eyes had been. He wasn't repulsed, but merely kissed me lightly and noted that I looked as if my IQ had dropped twenty points during the night.

He married me because I hung a magnetized potholder on his apartment door for his birthday and it stuck and looked very silly. He called to tell me he had found it and I knew that he would marry me.

Where is that charming child of yesterday? Where is her charming suitor? Gone the way of all flesh. Leaving something different, maybe better in that place.

It could be, you know, that with all my bitching, with all my dismal projections, that mine (and not the Duchess') is the love story of the century.